THE MEN IN THE MUSTARD HATS

THE MEN IN THE MUSTARD HATS

Gregory Spalding

Word Association Publishers
205 Fifth Avenue
Tarentum, PA, 15084

ISBN: 1-932205-08-X
Library of Congress Control Number: 2002114030

Word Association Publishers
205 Fifth Avenue,
Tarentum, PA 15084
www.wordassociation.com

Marketed and Distributed by:
City of Champions Publishing
Box 17276
Pittsburgh, Pennsylvania 15235
Phone and Fax: 412-829-5442
Email: concourseb@aol.com

DEDICATION

I DEDICATE THIS BOOK TO MANNY SANGUILLEN AND JOSE PAGAN, TWO OF MY FAVORITE PEOPLE CONNECTED WITH THESE PIRATE TEAMS WHO INSPIRED ME TO LEARN SPANISH, FOLLOW THE LORD AND TO ENJOY LIFE

YET I ALSO WISH TO HONOR EVERYONE CONNECTED WITH THESE PIRATE TEAMS WHO HELPED THEM BECOME A MODEL FRANCHISE FOR MAJOR LEAGUE BASEBALL AT THIS SPECIAL TIME IN PITTSBURGH HISTORY

ACKNOWLEDGMENTS

Cover artwork by Rita Lee Spalding

Firstly, I wish to thank my dear mother, Rita Spalding, for her excellent artwork featured on the cover of this book. It's a special privilege to work on a project of this magnitude with your very own mother. How many sons can say that about their mothers? I love you mom!

Secondly, I thank Sally O'Leary, Milt May and many of the other Pirates who contributed to the process through interviews and surveys.

Thirdly, the author also wishes to thank Sally O'Leary for permission to use photos and stats from the old yearbooks of that special time in Pirate baseball.

INTRODUCTION

Baseball, more than any other sport, connects people's histories, their past, present and future in an unbelievable way. You can go to a game in a modern stadium and something there will trigger a thought of the past, inspire you in the present and motivate you for the future. That's just the nature of the sport - it's connectivity if you will.

For that reason, this book continues my series on the Pirates of the '70's, one of those unique times in the history of Pirate baseball. The Buccos won five division titles in six years and a World Series from '70-'75, when they wore the mustard-colored hats. Hence this book gets its title from that reality.

My first two books in the series dealt with the super teams- the '71 World Champions and the '72 squad that many considered the finest in baseball that year.

This book, however, deals with the transition of the Buccos, when the Pirates had to reshape the roster and get back on track to the divisional titles.

In that transitional year of 1973, I see a connection with the present. Manny Sanguillen, the catcher on that team who also played rightfield, now owns a restaurant in PNC Park. Whenever I see him, he reminds me of these special days in Pirate baseball, when the Buccos were the best squad in the land. Art Howe, a Pittsburgh native who played with the Pirates in '74 and '75, returned to Pittsburgh as manager of the Oakland A's in June of 2002. Dave Parker also served as a short term coaching consultant for the Pirates in spring training in 2002. So those connections truly motivated me to pursue this project.

Yet that year of 1973 was difficult with the death of Clemente and the retirement of Mazeroski, among many other factors. Players such as Jim Rooker, Dal Maxvill, Richie Zisk and Dave Parker came onto the scene. The Pirates fell just short of winning another divisional pennant. But their year of transition allowed them to retool for two more divisional titles in 1974 and 1975. They also stayed very competitive throughout the rest of the decade.

The years of 1974 and 1975 brought two more divisional titles to the Buccos and a lot of new players such as Ken Brett, Jerry Reuss, John Candelaria, Ed Kirkpatrick, Larry Demery, Sam McDowell, Kent Tekulve and many others. It was an exciting time to see the team develop again under the watchful eye of Joe L. Brown. Current Oakland Manager Art Howe was a member of that team!

I'm even reminded of connections with the past in my family. After I married Lilly, I gained a sister-in-law with the name of Estella Mendoza from Mexico, who immediately reminded me of Mario Mendoza. My wife and son enjoy talking with the former latin players on the Pirates at card shows and other events. I have a photo of my son Carlos in front of the Mexico display at Cooperstown!

But rarely has anyone celebrated this special time in Pirate history. It was a special time of accomplishment that will never be matched again. The 5 division titles in 6 years is every bit as impressive as the 4 Super Bowls the Steelers won in 6 years.

There were so many unique moments, players and characters to cherish. Enjoy cherishing these special moments with me!

TABLE OF CONTENTS

1973 Schedule

Legend:
HOME ☐ ROAD ☐
☾—Night Games
☾☾—Twi Night Doubleheader
●●—Doubleheader
▶—11:05 a.m.
▶◀—10:35 a.m.
(L)—Ladies Days
(SC)—Senior Citizens Days

PROMOTION Days
Monday, May 28—Jersey Day (Memorial Day)
Friday, June 29—Wrist Band Night
Friday, July 20—Cap Night
Sunday, Aug. 12—Pennant Day
Sunday, Sept. 30—Fan Appreciation Day (Prize Day)

A STRANGER YEAR THERE COULDN'T BE THAN 1973

Pirate baseball historians will readily agree that 1973 stands as one of the most unique and bizarre seasons, both negatively and positively. Not only did the Pirates experience tragedy and strangeness but they also had some great accomplishments.

To start with, everyone had to deal with the death of Roberto Clemente. His departure created a serious void in leadership that would ultimately be Stargell's calling. But for a while in 1973, no one truly sensed direction.

Bill Mazeroski went from playing second base to coaching third base, a big transition for the 17-year player. That had to create some interesting moments during the year.

Joining Maz in the coaching chores would be Mel Wright as the pitching coach, Dave Ricketts in the bullpen and Don Leppert at first.

Parker and Zisk spent significant time in the majors adjusting to the way of life and the performance expectations. Both of them proved to be worthy additions with their incredible hitting prowess.

Furthermore, Al Oliver had his finest year with 20 homers 99 rbis and a .292 batting average to show that he had truly arrived as an all-around hitter.

Willie Stargell compiled his best year ever as he lead the league with 44 homers, 119 rbis, 43 doubles and in slugging percentage. He should have won the league mvp award over Pete Rose.

Yet two of the weirdest things that happened focused on Steve Blass and Bill Virdon. Steve Blass finished with a 3-9 record and a 9.81 era and completely lost his touch as one of the finest hurlers in the game. Bill Virdon got fired by Joe L.Brown late in the season, a move that Brown later admitted was his biggest mistake ever.

The season ended with a game against San Diego at Three Rivers after the season was over, part of a unique tiebreaker system.

Then you had several trades.

So, all in all, it was a weird year.

Before the season began, every single writer asked everyone how the team could and would function in the wake of Clemente's death. Reportedly, writers asked Willie Stargell so much about Roberto that he got to the point where he refused to talk about it anymore.

The most interesting aspect of the exhibition season focused on the advent of the designated hitter rule as the Twins' Larry Hisle, a Portsmouth native just like Al Oliver, became the first official practitioner of the craft on March 6th. He made the AL look good with two homeruns and seven rbi against the Bucco pitchers.

Naturally, the Buccos focused on reloading for another run at a division title the rest of the spring as they searched for a new rightfielder and leadership. They finished spring training with a 12-15 record and a .444 winning percentage. Bob Robertson impressed everyone with his .391 average for the spring.

Yet, as tragic and as sad as Clemente's death was, the Buccos still had to move on.

That's why before the Pirates could play their April 6th opener at Three Rivers, they had to retire Roberto's number. That symbolic act would bring closure to all of the sad feelings people carried with them.

Before the ceremony, Vera Clemente sat in the dugout and didn't talk to anyone. Then officials asked her to come to the microphone. Dressed in an elegant gray suit with a long skirt, she struggled with her emotions.

National League President Emeritus Warren Giles presented Vera with a gold lifetime Major League pass. Pirate GM Joe L. Brown then presented her with Roberto's 12th Gold Glove as one of the National League's top defensive outfielders.

During the retirement ceremony, the Buccos gave Roberto's last road uniform to his mother and his last home uniform to his wife. Somehow that served fitting. It was a touching moment to see Roberto's last triumph on a baseball field. Pirate President Dan Galbreath handled the retirement ceremonies and he declared,"May God be with you always," when he gave the uniforms to the respective ladies. Vera cried when she looked at her three sons and her mother-in-law.

Many of the 51,695 fans who attended this opening day fought back the tears on this emotional day, as they watched Roberto's wife, Vera Clemente, his mother, Mrs. Luisa Clemente, and his three sons-Roberto Jr, Luis and Enrique accept various gifts and appreciations on behalf of "The Great One". The fans gave her a standing ovation.

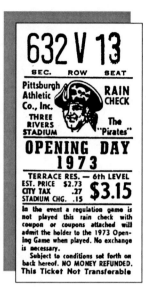

Senator Ruth Fernandez sang the Puerto Rican national anthem before the traditional Star-Spangled Banner.

Then the post-Clemente era began on the field for the Pirates against Bob Gibson and the St Louis Cardinals. It seemed weird watching a Buccos game without Clemente. Yet Richie Hebner summed it up best when he declared that we shouldn't mope about Roberto.

Yet the Buccos quickly fell behind 5-0 as Steve Blass rushed in his delivery and didn't have command of his pitches. The Cardinals took advantage of the situation.

Blass gave up the three second-inning tallies on four safeties, which included rbi singles by Bernie Carbo and Lou Brock and a sacrifice fly by Gibson.

The other two runs came on back-to-back force plays with the bases loaded, which followed a single by Ted Sizemore, a bases on balls and a hit batsman.

Al Oliver, however, broke Bob Gibson's shutout in the sixth inning with a sacrifice fly.

Then Hebner, true to his word, homered after missing the take sign from third-base coach Bill Mazeroski. Richie jokingly affirmed, "I forgot to look down at the Polack." That cut the lead to 5-2 in the seventh frame. Bill Virdon admitted that he forgave players for missing signs if they hit homers!

The home half of the eighth inning changed the whole momentum of the game as the Buccos knocked out Bob Gibson. Manny Sanguillen and Al Oliver singled and Stargell walked to load the bases. Riche Hebner followed with a two-run bloop double against reliever Diego Segui. Pinch-hitter Gene Clines tripled to drive home two more runs and give the Buccos a 6-5 lead. Ray Busse, a rookie shortstop with the Cardinals, then committed an error that allowed Clines to score the seventh run.

Lefthanded relievers Luke Walker, Jim Rooker and Ramon Hernandez shut down St Louis in the last four frames to clinch the triumph. Newcomer Jim Rooker got the win. Ramon Hernandez picked up the save.

Fittingly, the final out came when Lou Brock flied out to Sanguillen, Clemente's closest friend on the team who replaced him at his position.

After the game, Blass admitted that the Pirates had to prove they could win without Roberto. This comeback went a long way toward doing that.

Their momentum continued as they took a doubleheader from the Cardinals on April 8th by scores of 4-3 and 5-3, as Giusti beat Granger in the opener and Ellis beat Spinks in the nightcap. That 3-0 start certainly looked good to everyone.

Bob Moose then defeated Ferguson Jenkins at Three Rivers the next day by a 6-0 score to bring the Buccos record to 4-0. Somehow the Pirates seemed ready for the new season without Mazeroski and Clemente, their two future hall-of-famers.

So now the Pirates went on the road for the first time and lost their first game on Saturday, April 14th, by a 6-4 score to the Montreal Expos in Parc Jarry, but then won the next day by an 8-3 mark.

The roadtrip continued with stops in St Louis and Chicago, two of the Buccos strongest division rivals.

At Busch Stadium, Steve Blass again matched up against Bob Gibson and the Buccos prevailed by a 4-3 score on April 17th while Bob Moose defeated Rick Wise the next day by an 8-2 mark to raise the Buccos' record to 7-1 with another modest 3-game win streak.

In a series at historic Wrigley Field, the Buccos lost two out of three to the Cubbies on April 21-23, winning 10-4 on the 22nd in the middle game while losing 10-9 and 11-3 in the other contests.

Yet, despite losing two out of three, the Buccos had a very respectable 8-3 record and looked ready to challenge for the division for the fourth straight season.

Then came the big losing streak, four games of which were at home, that culminated with one of the most incredible losses in major league history.

The Padres came to town and defeated the Pirates 7-5 as Steve Arlin started against Bob Moose.

Those Los Angeles Dodgers, known for their incredible pitching, then won three consecutive one-run decisions against the Buccos by scores of 3-2, 9-8 and 2-1 as Don Sutton, Andy Messersmith and Claude Osteen outhurled Nellie Briles, Dock Ellis and Steve Blass on the 28th and 29th of April. That brought the losing streak to five games.

Their April record stood at 8-7, 2.5 games out of first place.

Then came one of the most incredible losses in major league history as the Pirates shouted, "Mayday", on the first of May. The Buccos lost their fourth consecutive one-run decision and their sixth overall game in Candlestick Park against the San Francisco Giants. But the circumstances of that loss amaze baseball historians and fans even to this day.

The Buccos cruised in this game with an 8-1 lead into the bottom of the ninth. The Buccos got two outs and Chris Speier was on first base for the Giants. It seemed like a pure formality to get the final out and break the losing streak. But this was more than a formality. Lead by Chris Arnold's pinch grand slam and Bobby Bonds' bases loaded two-bagger, the Giants tallied an NL-record tying seven markers in the bottom of the ninth to win, 8-7.

Everyone connected with the Pirates, from Bob Prince to the pitchers to the batboy to the fan at home listening on the radio, simply stood there in total disbelief. How can a team lose a seven-run lead in the bottom of the ninth after two outs?

Yet that losing streak and that loss seemed to sum up the season for the Pirates. They struggled to stay at or near .500 for the rest of the season and never regained their dominance of past years.

Showing their resilience, the Buccos did put together a nice three-game winning streak with two victories against the Giants in San Francisco by scores of 2-1 and 14-5 and then a 12-6 triumph in Jack Murphy Stadium to raise their record to 11-8. In that 14-5 win, Al Oliver collected four hits, which included two straight homers and six rbi. Rennie Stennett had six rbi in the 12-6 victory and clubbed two roundtrippers.

Yet, right after that, they lost two more in a row to drop to 11-10, losing 6-5 and 8-0 to the Padres, who ended up winning 60 games for the whole year.

That created a pattern of winning streaks and losing streaks that plagued the Buccos the rest of the season.

On May 7th and 8th at Dodger Stadium, the Pirates showed their real power. Five Pirates slammed solo homeruns in a 5-4 triumph on the 7th as Luke Walker outdueled Don Sutton. Then Willie Stargell made more history with his windmill stroke as he slammed a 470-foot roundtripper against Andy Messersmith that hit the rightfield pavilion roof, which became his second homer to leave Dodger Stadium. Although the Pirates lost 7-4, everyone marveled at Stargell's blast.

Things got worse as the Buccos lost to the Dodgers by an 8-5 count on May 9th and then came home to Three Rivers Stadium to lose four more consecutive contests.

That added up to another six-game losing streak and plummeted their record to 12-16.

Besides the two losses to the Dodgers, the Buccos also dropped three straight to the Mets, which included a 6-0 shutout against Tom Seaver, and one to the Expos.

How could the Pirates experience such losing streaks at home?

What a strange year unfolded!

The Pirates went on to win one, lose one, win one and lose one again. Then they won two and then followed that up with two losses.

Naturally, they followed that up with a 7-2 loss on May 25th against the Astros and future Pirate Jerry Reuss, and a win on May 26th by an identical 7-2 mark as Nellie Briles defeated Ken Forsch. The Buccos had a 17-20 record and were 6.5 games out of first.

But then, just as people got sick of the mediocrity, the Buccos put together a real streak..

After a 6-2 loss to Houston on May 27th, the Pirates closed out May with 4 consecutive wins to reach a 21-21 record.

Many things happened in the streak. On May 28th, Dock Ellis ended his five-game losing streak in defeating Don Wilson by a 4-2 count. Willie Stargell slammed his thirteenth circuit clout of the season in a 6-1 victory over the Braves. In another 4-2 triumph, this one on the 30th, the Buccos moved up to second place in the division. The final day of May saw Willie Stargell lambaste a Gary Gentry delivery into the upper deck for one of his famous homers that had a number sign for years to come. That number three served as a monument to that shot for years to come. Stargell's fourteenth homer lead the majors and also lead the Pirates back to .500.

The Buccos finished at 13-14 for the month but looked ready to move.

June started with two more wins to raise the winning streak to six, as the Buccos defeated the Reds by scores of 9-6 and 4-3 behind the pitching of Blass and Ellis to raise their record to 23-21. Stargell launched his fifteenth homer in the June 1st victory.

Then, on June 3rd, the Reds defeated the Pirates to end the streak, as Tony Perez' 3rd inning grand slam stood as the key blow in the 5-1 Cincinnati triumph with Clay Carroll defeating Luke Walker.

That precipitated another big losing streak.

Stargell slammed his sixteenth homer on June 4th but the Buccos still lost to the Giants by a 7-2 score.

The Giants triumphed again by a 3-2 score on June 5th behind Ron Bryant.

Then came a sad day as Steve Blass only lasted two innings in the June 6th 9-7 loss to the Giants at Three Rivers. Virdon hinted that Blass might have to move into the bullpen for a while.

After that loss, the Pirates had an off day and pondered their dilemma. What sense did it make that in their three biggest losing streaks so far, the majority of the losses came at the friendly confines of Three Rivers Stadium? What was wrong with Blass? Where was the leadership?

Yet the offday didn't help. The Astros defeated the Pirates by a 4-3 mark, despite Stargell's seventeenth homer, and the Pirates losing streak rose to five while their record fell to 23-26.

But things actually got worse. Perhaps Bob Robertson's .308 average was the only good news.

After a 4-1 victory over the Astros on June 9th, the Pirates fell into another five-game losing streak. Astro hurler Jerry Reuss defeated the Buccos 7-1 on June 10th, then the Pirates lost three to the Braves in Atlanta by 9-7, 4-2 and 18-3 marks. Those losses dropped them into fifth place and meant that they had lost nine out of their last ten.

Thankfully, the Pirates had an offday on June 14th.

So the next day Cincinnati's Fred Norman shut out the Buccos by a 6-0 tally. That was his first start as a Red after a trade with San Diego. This loss dropped the Pirates record to 24-31. In this rain-delayed game, Virdon made some changes by returning Sanguillen to catcher, benching May and putting Clines in rightfield. After the Pirates fifth straight loss, they found themselves 9.5 games out of first place.

Steve Blass #28

Nellie Briles stopped the bleeding the next day with a much-needed 5-0 shutout of the Reds at Riverfront Stadium.

Yet the Pirates fell even further the next day as they lost a June 17th doubleheader to the Cincinnati Reds by 3-1 and 5-1 scores. Luke Walker and Tom Dettore lost to Jack Billingham and Ross Grimsley. This defeat dropped the Buccos 10.5 games out of first place or a half-game out of the cellar, depending on your perspective. Stargell slammed his nineteenth roundtripper.

Then the Buccos rebounded by defeating Ferguson Jenkins by a 3-1 score at Three Rivers Stadium as Dock Ellis outhurled him. For some inexplicable reason, Jenkins had an unbelievable string of six straight 20-win seasons and ended up in Cooperstown, yet he couldn't beat the Buccos, even in this strange season! Yet the Bucs also won the nightcap of the doubleheader by a 4-3 score. But the Buccos ended up in the cellar after the day's action, a process that saw them go from first place on May 7th to sixth place on June 19th.

The Buccos closed out the series with the Cubs with a 5-3 loss to Rick Reuschel on June 20th and awaited the Mets arrival into town for a four-game series.

That first game on the 21st, a matchup of lefthanders Jerry Koosman and Luke Walker, ended in dramatic fashion in the bottom of the ninth. The Pirates and Mets had a 1-1 tie in the bottom of the ninth and the Pirates had the bases loaded. Tug McGraw, who admits to this day that Three Rivers Stadium stands as one of his least favorite places in the major leagues due to his failures there, then went to a 3-2 count on Bob Robertson and the big readhead hit the ball to second baseman Felix Millan. Millan forced out Gene Clines at the plate but the return throw to first base by the catcher ended up in rightfield. The rightfielder threw to Jim Fregosi who tagged out Al Oliver going to second base. Dave Cash, who stood on second base before the play started, then raced to third and home. Jim Fregosi frantically tried to throw Cash out at the plate but the fleet infielder made it home by a step. So the Three Rivers Stadium crowd went home deliriously happy with a wild victory. It was a badly needed victory.

On the 22nd, the Buccos fell back into a tie with the Phillies for last place as they dropped a 5-4 decision to New York. Steve Blass lasted only 2 2/3 innings and yielded five runs in the second.

Everyone wondered what happened to Blass. This became something much more serious than a slump. Blass admitted that he wondered if he was doing sixteen different things wrong mechanically and admitted that he didn't feel the same as when he was successful. Reportedly, he started reading books on positive thinking because his first twelve starts all had the same pattern of ineptitude. How does an all-star and a world series star suddenly find himself unable to find the plate?

On the 23rd, the Buccos rebounded to defeat the Mets in 10 innings by a 3-2 score.

But the up and down pattern continued with a 5-2 loss to Tom Seaver the next day that dropped them 10 games out of first place once again. Willie Stargell collected his 22nd homer to continue his amazing season. But the lowlight of the game occurred when Fernando Gonzalez, a utility third baseman, had a temper tantrum in the clubhouse when Gene Alley substituted for Richie Hebner at third base instead of him. He upset boxes sitting on a table near the trainer's room and also threw the stool that sat in front of his locker. Little did he know that he would be traded later in the year.

So the June 25th doubleheader sweep of the Montreal Expos at Parc Jarry certainly raised the spirits of everyone in the clubhouse as Bob Johnson and Nelson Briles lead the way to triumphs by scores of 8-6 and 3-1. Since success in doubleheaders stood as one of the main reasons for the Pirates' success in '72, many people thought the Pirates could get out of their slump.

On June 26th, the Expos thrashed the Pirates, 10-3. Steve Blass, who came in as a reliever, hurled 3 1/3 frames and faced seventeen men. Nine batters reached base against Blass, five on hits and four on walks. The questions about Blass grew more desperate and more serious.

The good thing was that the Pirates returned home on June 27th for a six-game homestand. But the bad thing was that the Buccos got destroyed for the second straight game. This time Jim Rooker took a pounding in the 15-4 loss to the St Louis Cardinals.

Curiously enough, it was Rooker's first start and he served up back-to-back gopher balls to Joe Torre and Ted Simmons in a six-run third. Blass relieved again and gave up one marker in the seventh frame and four in the ninth. In the Cardinals 22-hit attack, Joe Torre, the NL MVP in 1971, hit for the cycle with a double in the first, a roundtripper in the third, a triple in the fourth and a single in the ninth. He also hit into a double play and walked in his six plate appearances. Interestingly enough, Torre asked Manager Red Schoendienst to pinch-run for him but he refused that request in the 8th. That allowed him to complete the cycle. Only two other batters ever hit for the cycle at Three Rivers after Joe Torre and they both performed the feat near the end of its existence.

Regrettably, the Buccos fell 11 games behind the frontrunners.

So Dock Ellis's 6-0 shutout of the Cardinals the next day buoyed the team's spirit and lifted them back out of the cellar. Willie Stargell clubbed his 23rd homer of the season and 300th of his career.

Montreal's Expos came to town for a four-game series and the Buccos promptly swept them. That naturally helped get the Buccos out of the doldrums.

Bob Moose followed up Dock Ellis' fine performance with a whitewashing of his own, a 4-0 triumph, against Ernie McAnally.

Then, Nellie Briles closed out the month of June with a 5-1 victory against Balor Moore.

Consequently, the Pirates went 13-18 during June and finished with a cumulative record of 34-39.

July started beautifully with another one of those patented Pirate doubleheader sweeps, as lefthanders Luke Walker and Jim Rooker combined to shut down the Expo bats at Three Rivers by 6-2 and 8-4 scores. The five-game winning streak lifted the Pirates to a 36-39 mark and into third place in the NL East.

Yet the Pirates followed up that doubleheader sweep by losing a doubleheader at Busch Stadium to the Cardinals on July 3rd by scores of 4-0 and 7-6. Willie Stargell made Pirate history with a grand slam in the nightcap, his 301st homer that tied him with Ralph Kiner at number one in Bucco history. But he didn't want to talk about that after dropping the double dip.

On Independence Day, the Buccos lost to the Cardinals again, this time by a 11-3 count.

Fortunately, former Cardinal Nellie Briles defeated St Louis 3-2 with a complete-game victory on July 5th. That salvaged something out of the series. Because of the problems at shortstop, the Buccos Joe L. Brown considered picking up Dal Maxvill because Oakland released him. He had playoff experience and stood as a smart ballplayer who might give stability to the struggling Pirates.

Dodger Stadium seemed even less friendly than Busch Stadium after Los Angeles swept the Pirates 3-2, 8-6 and 3-2 behind the hurling of Don Sutton, Andy Messersmith and Tommy John. The Buccos dropped back into fifth place and desperately needed an offday.

So the offday on July 9th meant a great deal to the Pirates, a time to reload and get rejuvenated. Part of that rejuvenation came in the form of Dal Maxvill, as Joe L. Brown consummated the deal to pick him up and he actually joined the team in San Diego. Nellie Briles spoke highly of Maxvill as a steadying influence in the infield when he played with him on the World Series teams of 1967 and 1968. Dave Giusti also spoke very highly of him. Dal Maxvill would make Joe L. Brown look good by getting four hits in his first six Pirate at bats.

Fortunately, the Buccos won 4-3 against the Padres the next day to end the three-game skid. Unfortunately, Gene Clines suffered what many considered a season-ending injury when he tore the ligaments in his right ankle when he tried to stop his slide going into second base. The Buccos therefore brought up Dave Parker from the minors to replace Clines on the roster, a player many thought would become a superstar because of his 1972 season in Salem of 22 homers, 101 rbi and a .310 batting average.

Stargell lead the Pirates to a big victory the next day with his 25th circuit clout and Nelson Briles hurled his seventh complete game. This 10-2 victory over the Padres gave the Buccos a little bit of momentum.

On July 12th, the winning streak continued behind the masterful pitching of Luke Walker and the hitting of Wilver Dornell Stargell in a 4-0 victory over San Diego and Clay Kirby. Wilver clubbed his 26th roundtripper. But Luke Walker had an unbelievable performance as he hurled a complete game five-hit shuout with five strikeouts and no walks. In fact, he rarely got a three-ball count on a batter. That got the Bucco record to 40-45.

But things got bad again in Candlestick Park, the windiest ballpark in the majors. The Buccos lost two out of three to the Giants, which included a 12-0 shutout at the hands of Juan Marichal, "The Dominican Dandy", in the finale.

The Pirates all relished the opportunity to return home.

Los Angeles greeted them with a 1-0 loss on July 16th and an 8-4 loss the next day as Don Sutton and Andy Messersmith again stymied the Bucco bats. But the Buccos rebounded to defeat the Dodgers 3-2 on the 18th behind Dock Ellis. Stargell had his 28th homer in the last game of the series.

One of the sidebars of the year focused on the relationship between Virdon and Richie

Hebner. Bill Virdon actually benched Richie Hebner for a couple of games because he felt he paid too much attention to the hecklers in the stadium and didn't concentrate enough on the game. Things would escalate between the two later on in the season.

In a strange twist of circumstances, the Pirates defeated the Padres in two doubleheaders, one on July 20th and another on July 22nd. This happened due to the inclement weather naturally. But that doesn't happen much in baseball.

In the July 20th doubleheader sweep, which included 5-4 and 7-0 victories, Stargell hit another four-bagger and Rennie Stennett collected seven hits in ten at bats, including two homers of his own.

Then the July 22nd sweep, which included 3-1 and 13-7 triumphs behind the hurling of Nellie Briles and Luke Walker, helped them finish with a 46-49 mark at the All-Star break. This five-game winning streak got them back into third place and they only trailed the first place team by 4.5 games. So they could feel good that they got themselves back into the race after trailing by 11 games earlier in the campaign.

The Sporting News published the all-star balloting and the Pirates did well. Stargell finished second at first base behind Hank Aaron. Richie Hebner finished fourth at the "hot corner." Manny Sanguillen placed second at catcher while Al Oliver finished seventh among outfielders.

Willie Stargell and Dave Giusti represented the Pirates at the All-Star Game in Royals Stadium in Kansas City on July 24th, the 40th anniversary of the mid-summer classic. Surviving members of the 1933 All-Star Game attended such as Carl Hubbell, Lefty Gomez, Lefty Grove, Joe Cronin and Charlie Gehringer. It also stood as Willie Mays' final appearance at the All-Star Game, whom many considered the greatest performer in all-star history. Dave Giusti hurled a scoreless seventh inning for the NL. Stargell got to bat against Nolan Ryan and that was power against power, a battle won this time by the flamethrowing righthander who struck Willie out. Bobby Bonds got the MVP Award as a result of his homer and double. The National League's 7-1 victory raised their record to 25-18-1 against the AL.

Stargell and Giusti rejoined their Pirate teammates in Chicago for a series with the Cubs and the winning streak increased to a season-best seven games with 3-2 and 10-6 triumphs behind Dock Ellis and Nellie Briles on the 26th and 27th. That brought them to a 48-49 record, only one game away from .500.

Then the Phillies came to Three Rivers Stadium, for the famous Pennsylvania rivalry. Philadelphia took the first game 5-0 behind Wayne Twitchell to drop the Buccos two games under .500 again.

A Pirate trademark, however, the doubleheader sweep, bailed the team out again on July 29th. Ironically, the Buccos won both games by identical 5-2 scores behind John Morlan and Luke Walker. Stargell walloped his 31st homer and Richie Zisk contributed a 4 for 4 game. The Pirates now stood at 50-50 and really looked ready to make a move.

But Steve Carlton shutout the Buccos the next day by a 1-0 count to put them under .500 again.

Fortunately, on the last day of July, Dock Ellis defeated Jerry Koosman by a 4-1 score at Shea Stadium and the Pirates evened their record at 51-51 once again.

That meant that the Pirates had their first winning month of the season with a 17-12 record during July. Perhaps that meant that they were ready to truly move up in the standings.

A three-game losing streak, which included a doubleheader loss on August 1st to the Mets at Shea by 3-0 and 5-2 scores, as Dal Maxvill had the only rbi of the day with a booming double. GM Joe L. Brown sent versatile Vic Davalillo, whose batting average had fallen to .181, to the Oakland Athletics for cash on the first. Gene Clines, who considered himself a close friend of Davalillo's, really felt sad to see him go.

A 5-1 loss on August 2nd took more wind out of the sails of the Pirate Ship.

But they rebounded to take three out of four from the Phillies at Veteran's Stadium, which included a 3-1 victory over Steve Carlton, an 11-5 loss to future Pirate Ken Brett, an 11-4 triumph over Jim Lonborg and a 4-1 win against Wayne Twitchell. So that brought them back to 54-55 on August 5th.

Monday, August 6th, stood as an incredibly emotional day for the whole Pirate family as Cooperstown officially inducted Roberto Clemente and five other players. Baseball's writers unanimously voted to waive the five-year rule and it was a difficult day for many of Roberto's teammates and family. Vera Clemente held the plaque during the ceremonies at Cooperstown and her sad disposition affected everyone. Stargell sat in the audience with a look of disbelief, as if he still couldn't come to grips with his teammate's death. Clemente became the first Latin-born player to enter the Hall of Fame.

In the actual Hall of Fame Game at Doubleday Field, the Texas Rangers beat the Pittsburgh Pirates, 6-4. In one of his most embarrassing moments of the season, Blass got removed from the Hall of Fame Game after only 2 2/3 innings of work. That had to really make Steve lose his confidence.

Then, after all that emotion, it was time to get back into the pennant race at Three Rivers with the 11-game homestand coming up.

On August 7th and 8th, the Houston Astros split a series with the Pirates as Houston won 2-0 and then Pittsburgh returned the favor with a 4-3 count. But the Pirates had to do better than splitting with teams. They had to make a move. They did find themselves in second place, only 4.5 games out. But they had to put another winning streak together.

The Braves came to town and took two out of three from the Pirates. Phil Niekro defeated Dock Ellis 5-4 on August 10th and then the Braves won again by a 9-3 score the next day. Bob Moose won the third game by a 5-2 margin and amazingly the Pirates stood only 3 games out and in second place. After that third game, things got rather ugly in the clubhouse as Manager Bill Virdon and Richie Hebner got into a shouting match when Richie took exception to the manager replacing him with Gene Alley late in the game for defensive purposes. Joe L. Brown called a press conference and then told the writers he had nothing to announce, a move that many felt signified that he didn't want people to think he fired Virdon due to the Hebner incident.

After Nellie Briles won by a 3-2 count on August 13th, the Buccos were only two games out. Maybe the Buccos would make the move now.

But then the Pirates seemed to fall down again with a three-game losing streak that dropped their record to 57-61. The Buccos lost 5-4 and 1-0 to the Reds and then 5-3 to the Giants. Despite the losing streak, the Pirates still resided in second place, only three games out.

On August 18th and 19th, the Pirates defeated the Giants by 6-5 and 5-0 scores. Jim Rooker, one of the Pirates best hitting pitchers over the years, collected three singles and hurled a five-hit shutout against Juan Marichal.

In this crazy division race of 1973, the Pirates went 5-6 in their eleven-game homestand and actually rose 3.5 games in the standings, gaining ground from 5.5 out to 2 out. Everyone wondered about that. But that gave the Pirates a lot of hope heading into the stretch run.

So it was time to go on the road again, this time to Houston, Atlanta and Cincinnati.

James Rodney Richard, that 6 foot 8 inch flamethrowing righthander, shut down the Pirate bats with a two-hitter in a 10-2 victory on August 20th in the Astrodome. Al Oliver broke up James Rodney Richard's no-hit bid.

But the Pirates bounced right back with victories the next two days by scores of 6-3 and 4-0. Bob Moose hurled the shutout and John Morland started the other game. The one negative was that Stargell got hit in the back of a neck by a pitch from Juan Pizarro in the shutout.

Now it was time for the trip to the launching pad, Atlanta Fulton County Stadium. The Buccos lost two out of three to the Braves, dropping the two bookend games by scores of

3-2 and 8-6 while winning the middle game by a count of 6-5. In that Pirate victory, Richie Hebner launched his 18th homer when he lead off the 11th frame to give the Buccos the win. Amazingly, the Buccos actually gained even more ground and stood only 1.5 games out.

Manager Bill Virdon acknowledged that there would be changes in the offseason.

At Riverfront on August 28th and 29th, the Pirates again split a series. Bob Moose and the Buccos beat the Reds 8-3 in the opener and then they defeated our Buccos 5-3 on the 29th. Bob Moose outhurled Ross Grimsely in the first one and Jack Billingham defeated Nellie Briles in the second contest.

The Pirates finished August against the Cubs at Three Rivers and they got back to the .500 mark once again by sweeping a doubleheader on the last day of the month. Jim Rooker shutout Rick Reuschel 7-0 in the opener and John Morlan defeated Ferguson Jenkins 5-2 in the nightcap as the Pirates evened their season record at 65-65.

Amazingly, the Pirates played exactly at .500 during the month of August with a 14-14 record.

September 1st started with a 1-0 shutout by Bruce Kison over Burt Hooton and the Cubs at Three Rivers to put the Pirates over .500 at 66-65. Willie Stargell, whom many thought had almost as good an arm as Clemente's, threw out Jose Cardenal trying to go from first to third. The Buccos then won in dramatic fashion in the bottom of the ninth. Gene Clines lead off with a single and then tried to steal second but the catcher threw him out. Hebner then singled. Oliver followed with a two-bagger and the place erupted. Stargell came to the plate and Burt Hooton decided to walk him intentionally to load the bases. Richie Zisk then stepped to the plate and worked Hooton to a 2-2 count before driving the next pitch into deep centerfield over the drawn in outfield. Three Rivers exploded!

But the Pirates dropped the game the next day to even their record once again. The Cubs defeated them 5-3.

In their infamous traditional Labor Day doubleheader, the Pirates split with the Cardinals on September 3rd. They defeated the Cardinals 5-4 in the opener and then lost the nightcap 8-3. Richie Hebner won the first game with an inside-the -park homer in the 13th frame.

The Pirates lost two more games at Three Rivers to the Cardinals by scores of 4-2 and 5-3. That dropped them to 67-69, two games under .500 again.

That September 4th 4-2 loss especially frustrated the Pirates because of the umpiring. In the eighth frame of that crucial contest, Dave Giusti threw a wild pitch on a 2-2 count to Tim McCarver with Lou Brock on third base. Naturally, even though it was a short wild pitch, the fleet-footed Brock attempted to score. The throw from Sanguillen, Giusti and Brock all arrived at the same time and Giusti made the tag. Eddie Vargo initially called Brock out even though Giusti dropped the ball. He obviously felt that Dave held the ball long enough for the putout. St Louis protested strongly, and after consulting with second base umpire Bruce Froemming, nicknamed "little Caesar", called Brock safe. Froemming ruled him safe and Vargo let that supersede his initial call. That turned out to be the Cardinals third run and turned the tide in the game.

People wondered if the Pirates would ever get out of their funk. Twenty-five games remained in the season and the Pirates only stood three games out. But they had to put a winning streak together that would get them over the top.

The Pirate GM pondered the situation on the offday of September 6th.

Then, at 4:30 PM on Thursday, September 6th, the strangest happening of the whole season took place when Joe L. Brown fired Bill Virdon and brought back Danny Murtaugh for the fourth time. Brown called it the most difficult decision he ever made in baseball and later, many years later, admitted that it was a mistake. But he thought he had to do something to change the fortunes of the team.

The move shocked most of the Pirate players. It also amazed fans and most people in baseball. Why would you fire a manager with so little time left in the season?

In the first two games under Murtaugh, the Pirates posted wins at Veteran's Stadium over the Phillies by scores of 10-8 and 5-3 to get back to .500 at 69-69. Bruce Kison and Bob Moose helped defeat Ken Brett and Steve Carlton. In the 5-3 triumph, Stargell drove in his 100th rbi and also scored the winning tally.

But the September 9th game stunned the Pirates as they lead the Phillies 7-1 going into the bottom of the seventh and lost 8-7. Philadelphia's Willie Montanez lead off the bottom of the ninth with a roundtripper to win the game. Stargell slammed his 39th homer in the losing effort.

In the 11-3 victory on September 10th, the Pirates got to within 1.5 games of first as Richie Zisk went 5 for 6 and Stargell raised his batting average to .305. Zisk also made a diving catch of Don Kessinger's line drive in the first inning, something that showed he could play rightfield well, as evidenced by his 12 assists during the course of the season while only committing two errors.

Steve Blass actually pitched well on September 11th as he only gave up two runs in a 2-0 loss to the Cubs. Randy Hundley hit a homer and the other run scored as the result of a Dal Maxvill error on a double-play ball. He still struggled but lasted five innings and only gave up two hits, five walks and hit one batter. After his horrible outings, this stood as something positive to build on.

Bob Robertson got back into the groove with a three-run homer on September 12th in a 4-2 victory over the Cubs at Wrigley Field. He felt good being back in the lineup regularly. The Buccos got back into first place with the victory.

With their 6-1 triumph over Milt Pappas and the Cubs on September 13th, the Pirates got back over .500 and looked like they would win their fourth consecutive division title. They would stay in first place for quite a few days down the stretch.

On September 14th, Nellie Briles again defeated his former team, the Cardinals, by a 3-2 score. The Buccos looked like a team ready to take control of the race down the stretch. In the first frame, the Pirates scored all their runs on a Parker single, an Al Oliver hbp, a Hebner double, a Milt May walk and a Robertson single. When Hebner attempted to score, catcher Ted Simmons jumped for the ball and somehow kicked Richie in the head. Hebner missed home plate and umpire Satch Davidson called him out. Hebner got thrown out of the game for arguing with the umpire and for spitting tobacco juice all over his face. Stargell did his best to restrain him but it didn't work. Bill Virdon drove from Springfield to have a farewell meeting with the team and wished them luck in winning another world championship.

The Pirates maintained their lead on the 15th with a 7-4 victory over the Cardinals and that gave them a four-game winning streak. Dave Parker came off the bench to hit an impressive three-run homer.

In the finale of the series, the Cardinals defeated a shaky Steve Blass and the Pirates 7-3. Blass truly struggled through six innings.

In their return to Three Rivers for a short series, the Pirates throttled the Mets 10-3 on September 17th and stretched their lead to 1.5 games. Willie Stargell knocked out four extra-base hits, including his 40th homer. Richie Hebner followed up Stargell's with one of his own in the third frame and that made the ninth time that the Buccos hit back-to-back homers.

When the Pirates lost to the Mets 6-5 on September 18th, they knew that they had let one get away. They couldn't afford to give games away like this. But that they did. The Mets trailed 5-1 heading into the top of the ninth at Three Rivers. Then they rallied for five tallies and won 6-5.

But the next two games made things even worse as the Pirates lost two more at Shea, by scores of 7-3 and 4-3. Stargell hit his 41st homer in the September 19th loss. In the September 20th 4-3 loss, the Buccos lost in 13 innings. Pirate Dave Augustine hit a controversial ball that hit off the fence and went into an outfielder's glove that could have been a homer. A key relay throw from Cleon Jones to Wayne Garrett to the catcher nailed Richie Zisk at home in the top of the final inning. The Pirates now had a 75-75 record after an ill-timed three game losing streak and held a slim .5 game lead.

On September 21st, the Pirates dropped out of first place and never recovered as Tom Seaver defeated the Pirates, 10-2. Blass started the game and five other pitchers saw action. The Mets had a 77-77 record and lead the Pirates (75-76) by 1.5 games.

After a rainout on September 22nd, the Pirates swept a doubleheader from the Expos by 6-3 and 7-4 scores in Parc Jarry as Bruce Kison and Dock Ellis both started. That raised their record back to 77-76 and got them back to within a half game of the lead.

Another doubleheader against the Expos yielded a split and the Pirates maintained their position. The Expos won the opener, 5-4, and the Pirates won the nightcap, 3-0, as Nellie Briles, the Pirates' most consistent pitcher, hurled a shutout. That 3-0 win served as a showcase for Stargell as he collected two hits in three at bats, including the game winning homer. Willie also reached over the fence to nab a potential game-tying homer by Ken Singleton. Then, in the seventh frame, he threw out a runner at the plate. The Buccos now had a 78-77 record.

Danny Murtaugh made the cover of Sports Illustrated on September 24th as the magazine featured the unique divisonal race in which every win or loss might mean two or three spots in the standings. People called the division the "National League Least" and the "Subtraction Division."

The Phillies then came to town to pay their crosstate rivals a visit. Steve Carlton defeated Jim Rooker by a 2-1 count on September 25th and the Mets also won. On September 26th, the Pirates exploded against Jim Lonborg for a 13-2 triumph and the Mets lost. So the Pirates trailed by a half game. The final game of the series saw the Phillies defeat the Pirates 3-2 as Greg Luzinski scored on a wild pitch in the 13th inning after catcher Bob Boone reached out to hit a pitch that relief pitcher Chris Zachary intended as an intentional walk. The Mets had an offday so the Buccos trailed by one full game heading into the final series of the season with a 79-79 record. The Mets were two games above .500.

That final series of the season came against the Montreal Expos at Three Rivers Stadium.

A distinct possibility arose of a three-way tie between Montreal, St Louis and Pittsburgh. This last weekend would be very interesting. The league declared that in the case of a three-way tie, Pittsburgh would play St Louis and then the winner would go on to face the Mets.

On Friday, September 28th, the Expos defeated the Pirates 3-2 and the Pirates dropped one game under .500.

Then, on September 29th, Nellie Briles started the game and then pulled himself out due to injury, after giving up a single to Mike Jorgensen. Jim McKee replaced him and finished out the inning. After a rain delay, Richie Hebner brought home Cash with the first run of the ballgame. The Expos, however, picked up five runs on the Pirate pitching staff. Stargell and Hebner then helped get Pittsburgh within two. But the Buccos ended up losing 6-4 as reliever Mike Marshall shut them down..

On the final day of the season, the Buccos thrashed the Expos 10-2. Jim Rooker got the win and the Pirates sported an 80-81 mark. But the win kept the Pirate hopes alive.

In one of the most bizarre finishes in baseball history, the Pirates had hope because the Mets doubleheader got rained out. So the season had to be extended one day.

The scenario unfolded this way. There could be a two-way tie, a three-way tie or New York could win it outright.

First of all, in a weird happening, the San Diego Padres came all the way east to make up a rainout from earlier in the season against the Pirates. That game could have a significant meaning in the race.

New York would clinch the title if they won one of their doubleheader games against the Cubs. There would be a three-way tie if New York lost two and Pittsburgh won. There could have been a two-way tie between New York and St Louis if New York lost two and Pittsburgh lost.

New York actually won the first game of their doubleheader by a score of 6-4 as Tom Seaver defeated Burt Hooton at Wrigley Field before the Pirates started playing on October 1st. So they won the division with a 82-79 record.

San Diego then defeated the Pirates 4-3 in a somewhat meaningless game as Randy Jones defeated Bruce Kison and the Pirates finished under .500 at 80-82 for the only time in the decade of the '70's. They finished 2.5 games behind the Mets(82-79) and a game behind the Cardinals(81-81). About 2,500 fans showed up for the finale.

One of the strangest seasons in Pirate history ended in one of the strangest ways ever.

1973 STATISTICS
TEAM BATTING

Team	Pct.	a/b	r	h	hr	sb
Atlanta	.266	5631	799	1497	206	84
Los Angeles	.263	5604	675	1473	110	109
San Francisco	.262	5537	739	1452	161	112
Pittsburgh	.261	5608	704	1465	154	23
St Louis	.259	5478	643	1418	75	100
Cincinnati	.254	5505	741	1398	137	148
Houston	.251	5532	681	1391	134	92
Montreal	.251	5369	668	1345	125	77
Philadelphia	.249	5546	642	1381	134	51
Chicago	.247	5363	614	1322	117	65
New York	.246	5457	608	1345	85	27
San Diego	.244	5457	548	1330	112	88

TEAM PITCHING

Team	ERA	G	IP	H	R	BB	SO
Los Angeles	3.00	162	1491	1270	565	461	961
St Louis	3.25	162	1461	1366	603	486	867
New York	3.26	161	1465	1345	588	490	1027
Cincinnati	3.40	162	1473	1389	621	518	801
Chicago	3.66	161	1438	1471	655	438	885
Montreal	3.73	162	1452	1356	702	681	866
Pittsburgh	3.73	162	1451	1426	693	564	839
Houston	3.75	162	1461	1389	672	575	907
San Francisco	3.79	162	1452	1442	702	485	787
Philadelphia	3.99	162	1447	1435	717	632	919
San Diego	4.16	162	1430	1461	770	548	845
Atlanta	4.25	162	1462	1467	774	575	803

NL INDIVIDUAL BATTING

Player	Pct.	a/b	r	h	hr	rbi	sb
Rose, Pete	.338	680	115	230	5	64	10
Cedeno, Cesar	.320	525	86	168	25	70	56
Maddox, Gary	.319	587	81	187	11	76	24
Perez, Tony	.314	564	73	177	27	101	3
Watson, Bob	.312	573	97	179	16	94	1
Simmons, Ted	.310	619	62	192	13	91	2
Cardenal, Jose	.303	522	80	158	11	68	19
Singleton, Ken	.302	560	100	169	23	103	2
Matthews, Gary	.300	540	74	162	12	58	17
Garr, Ralph	.299	668	94	200	11	55	35
Stargell, Willie	.299	522	106	156	44	119	0
Fairly, Ron	.298	413	70	123	17	49	2
Brock, Lou	.297	650	110	193	7	63	70
Crawford, W	.295	457	75	135	14	66	12
Lum, Mike	.294	513	74	151	16	82	2
Oliver, Al	.292	654	90	191	20	99	6

NL INDIVIDUAL PITCHING

Pitcher	W-L	ERA	G	IP	H	BB	SO
Seaver, Tom	19-10	2.07	36	290	219	64	251
Sutton, Don	18-10	2.43	33	256	196	56	197

Twitchell, Wayne	13-9	2.50	34	223	172	99	169
Marshall, Mike	14-11	2.66	92	179	163	74	124
Messersmith, Andy	14-10	2.70	33	250	196	77	177
Gibson, Bob	12-10	2.77	25	195	159	57	142
Renko, Steve	15-11	2.81	36	250	201	108	164
Briles, Nelson	14-13	2.84	33	219	201	51	94
Koosman, Jerry	14-15	2.84	35	263	234	76	156
Roberts, Dave	17-11	2.86	39	249	264	62	119
Rooker, Jim	10-6	2.86	41	170	143	52	122
Reuschel, Rick	14-15	3.00	36	237	244	62	168
Cleveland, Reggie	14-10	3.01	32	224	211	61	122
Billingham, Jack	19-10	3.04	40	293	257	95	155
Ellis, Dock	12-14	3.05	28	192	176	55	122

PIRATE HITTING

Player	g	a/b	h	2b	3b	hr	bb	o	rbi	pct.
Zisk, Richi	103	333	108	23	7	10	21	63	54	.324
Stargell, Willie	148	522	156	43	3	44	0	129	119	.299
Oliver, Al	158	654	191	38	7	20	22	52	99	.292
Parker, Dave	54	139	40	9	1	4	2	27	14	.288
Augustine, Dave	11	7	2	1	0	0	1	0	0	.286
Sanguillen, Manny	149	589	166	26	7	12	17	9	65	.282
Hebner, Richie	144	509	138	28	1	25	56	60	74	271
Cash, Dave	116	436	118	21	2	2	38	36	31	271
May, Milt	101	283	76	8	1	7	34	26	31	269
Clines, Gene	110	304	80	11	3	1	26	36	23	.263
McNertney, Jerry	9	4	1	0	0	0	0	0	0	250
Hernandez, Jackie	54	73	18	1	2	0	4	2	8	.247
Stennett, Rennie	28	466	113	18	3	10	16	63	55	.242
Robertson, Bob	119	397	95	16	0	14	55	70	40	.239
Gonzalez, Fernando	37	49	11	0	1	1	5	1	11	.224
Alley, Gene	76	158	32	3	2	2	20	28	8	203
Maxvill, Dal	74	217	41	4	3	0	22	40	17	.189
Davalillo, Vic	59	*	*	*	*	1	*	*	3	.181
Campanis, Jim	6	6	1	0	0	0	0	0	0	.167

PIRATE PITCHING

Pitcher	G	W-L	IP	H	R	ER	BB	SO	ERA
Foor, Jim	3	0-0	1.1	2	0	0	1	1	0.00
Giusti, Dave	67	9-2	99	89	31	26	37	64	2.36
Hernandez, Ramon	59	4-5	90	71	27	24	25	64	2.40
Briles, Nelson	36	14-13	219	201	*	*	51	94	2.84
Rooker, Jim	41	10-6	170	143	59	54	52	22	2.85
Zachary, Chris	6	0-1	12	10	*	*	1	6	3.00
Ellis, Dock	28	12-14	192	176	86	65	55	122	3.05
Kison, Bruce	7	3-0	44	36	17	15	24	26	3.07
Moose, Bob	33	12-13	201	219	86	79	70	111	3.54
Johnson, Bob	50	4-2	92	98	*	*	34	68	3.62
Morlan, John	10	2-2	41	42	18	18	23	23	3.95
Walker, Luke	37	7-12	122	120	*	*	66	74	4.65
McKee, Jim	15	0-1	27	31	*	*	17	3	5.67
Dettore, Tom	12	0-1	22.2	33	*	*	14	13	5.96
Lamb, John	21	0-1	29.2	37	*	*	10	11	6.07
Blass, Steve	23	3-9	89	109	98	97	84	27	9.81

General Manager Joe L. Brown

AN OFFSEASON OF REFLECTION AND CHANGE

After winning three division titles and a world championship in three years, missing the playoffs didn't sit well with people in the Pirate organization. They realized that with their talent they had the potential for a dynasty.

So they learned from their mistake of 1973. After missing the World Series due to a wild pitch and seeing two future Hall-of-Famers no longer a part of the team, the Bucco brass should have done more to prepare for the transitional year of 1973. Their unwillingness to make moves to improve the club inevitably cost them another division title. After all, only a late season slump in the last week of the season ousted them from postseason play for the first time in three seasons.

Before the World Series ended, Joe L. Brown made his first deal as he sent second baseman Dave Cash to Philadelphia for pitcher Ken Brett. With Rennie Stennett's development and Willie Randolph around, the Pirates considered dealing Cash a good move. Brett, a lefthander, promised to improve the pitching staff as he posted major league highs with 13 wins, 25 starts, 10 complete games, 212 innings pitched and an era of 3.44. He also stood as an excellent fielder while handling 52 chances without an error. On top of that, he hit the ball extremely well, having hit four homers in four consecutive games.

Brown followed that with a deal on October 31st for another lefthander by sending catcher Milt May to Houston for pitcher Jerry Reuss. That would turn out to be a great deal for the Pirates as Reuss became the ace of the staff. Reuss' 1973 season prompted Joe L. Brown to make the move as he set career highs with 16 wins, 41 games, 40 starts, 12 complete games, 279 innings pitched, 177 strikeouts and a 3.74 era. Although the Pirates would miss May, the best second-string catcher in all of baseball, they desperately needed pitching.

Now all fans awaited the announcement of the National League MVP voting on Wednesday, November 21st, an annual rite for the baseball writers. Willie Stargell had his career-best year in 1973 as he lead both leagues in six different categories- homers(44), rbi(119), doubles(43), slugging percentage(.646), game-winning hits and extra-base hits. On top of that, he almost batted .300 as he finished at .299. Few people have ever had such a year. Yet the writers gave it to Pete Rose, who lead both leagues in only one area-batting average. That truly felt like a slap in the face to Stargell. Who in the world deserved it more than him? To be honest, although he deserved the award in 1979 as well, he deserved it more in '73 than in any other. In the American League, Reggie Jackson got the MVP with far inferior stats to Stargell's. Everyone called it a controversial vote, but Rose edged out Stargell. Everyone connected with the Pirates looked at the writer's decision with incredulity.

So, after that disappointment, Brown got busy with another trade on December 4th, as he sent Nellie Briles and hothead Fernando Gonzalez to Kansas City for Ed Kirkpatrick, a hustling first baseman-catcher-outfielder with the nickname "Spanky", Kurt Bevaqua, another hustler and minor league 1B Winston Cole. That deal would help bring more hustle and desire to the squad.

In a short amount of time, the general manager had changed the complexion of the team considerably. This would help the Pirates retool for another run at the division title the following year,

Reflecting on the positives for 1973, you had to immediately think of the three lefthanded sluggers who had their best power years ever, Willie Stargell, Al Oliver and Richie Hebner. Stargell, as mentioned above, had his career year. Yet Al Oliver also had his best year with 20 homers and 99 rbi, something that truly placed him in the elite hitters of the league. Richie Hebner had an incredible season with 25 roundtrippers. So the lefthanded sluggers would provide a great foundation for the future.

Regrettably, however, only one regular hit over .300 for the year, as Richie Zisk sported a .324 batting average. The rest of the Pirate hitters performed well below their career averages, which caused them to lose many games they should have won.

Two real positives came in the form of two outfielders named Richie Zisk and Dave Parker, who both performed extremely well and would both end up being 100-rbi men for the Pirates in the future.

On the negative side, the starting pitching really fell apart as only one full-time starter had a winning record and that was only by one game- Nellie Briles at 14-13. Jim Rooker sported a 10-6 mark but split time between starting and relieving. So Joe L. Brown did the right thing by trading for starting pitchers.

Steve Blass, who gave up an NL worst 84 walks in 89 innings, went to the Florida Instructional League after the season to work on his hurling.

The relief pitching stood in the capable hands of Dave Giusti with 20 saves and a 2.37 era and Ramon Hernandez with 11 saves and a 2.41 era. That served as a consistent carryover from the previous season.

Although the Pirates just missed qualifying for the playoffs for the fourth straight year, observers and team officials all knew that they truly underperformed. The Pirates dropped to fourth in team batting average with a .261 mark and tied with the Montreal Expos for sixth place in team era with a 3.73 rating. Only one batter made the top ten in batting and only two made the top fifteen. So the Buccos had some work to do to get back to the top.

After the first of the new year, Joe L. Brown made still another deal by sending Jackie Hernandez to the Phillies for catcher Mike Ryan. That would provide the Pirates with a reliable backup that they lost when they dealt May to Houston.

Mike Ryan   **#5**

Four of the Players the Pirates Tried at Shortstop in 1974

Frank Taveras   #10

Dave Popovich   #24

Dal Maxvill   #11

Kurt Bevacqua   #14

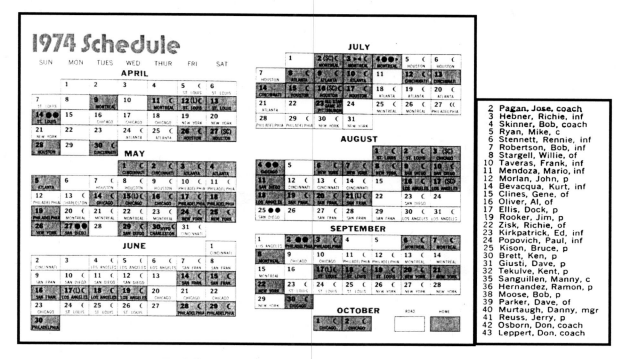

1974 Schedule

Players roster:

2 Pagan, Jose, coach
3 Hebner, Richie, inf
4 Skinner, Bob, coach
5 Ryan, Mike, c
6 Stennett, Rennie, inf
7 Robertson, Bob, inf
8 Stargell, Willie, of
10 Taveras, Frank, inf
11 Mendoza, Mario, inf
12 Morlan, John, p
14 Bevacqua, Kurt, inf
15 Clines, Gene, of
16 Oliver, Al, of
17 Ellis, Dock, p
19 Rooker, Jim, p
22 Zisk, Richie, of
23 Kirkpatrick, Ed, inf
24 Popovich, Paul, inf
25 Kison, Bruce, p
30 Brett, Ken, p
31 Giusti, Dave, p
32 Tekulve, Kent, p
35 Sanguillen, Manny, c
36 Hernandez, Ramon, p
38 Moose, Bob, p
39 Parker, Dave, of
40 Murtaugh, Danny, mgr
41 Reuss, Jerry, p
42 Osborn, Don, coach
43 Leppert, Don, coach

SOMETHING MORE IN '74

After the disappointment of falling short and with all of the offseason changes, a new optimistic spirit permeated the Pirate squad in the spring of 1974. The franchise looked forward to many special moments with the addition of many new people on the roster and the prospect of hosting the mid-summer classic as well. So everyone looked forward to the Pirates getting back on track.

Most baseball observers thought the Pirates had a dynasty in the making with the Lumber Company of Al Oliver, Richie Zisk, Willie Stargell, Richie Hebner, Manny Sanguillen, Bob Robertson and many others. The offseason acqusitions strengthened the pitching staff with Jerry Reuss, Jim Rooker, Ken Brett, newcomer Larry Demery and mainstay Dock Ellis. The bullpen featured Dave Giusti and Ramon Hernandez as well as Bruce Kison and John Morlan. Other players on the roster included Gene Clines, Ed Kirkpatrick, Dave Parker, Mario Mendoza, Paul Popovich, Art Howe, Kurt Bevacqua, Mike Ryan, Dal Maxvill, Dave Augustine, Chuck Brinkman, Ken Macha, Ed Ott and Miguel Dilone.

Only Don Leppert remained with the coaching staff as Bob Skinner took over at thirdbase and batting instructor, Jose Pagan became the firstbase coach/infield instructor and Don Osborn returned as pitching mentor. Leppert switched from firstbase to the bullpen and catching duties.

Spring training of 1974 didn't go well for the Buccos as they had a 10-15 record and a .400 winning percentage. Many fans feared that this would translate into the regular season. But everyone knows that spring training stands as a time to get ready for the new season.

Joe L. Brown showed his commitment to improve the team once again by sending pitcher Tom Dettore to the Chicago for shortstop Paul Popovich, whose claim to fame focused on his once having played basketball on the WVU team with Jerry West. So the Pirates had a real abundance of shortstops with the retirement of Gene Alley and the trade of Jackie Hernandez.

So, in very short order, the Pirate equipped themselves with a new arsenal that would help them get back to the top of the division after that short detour in 1973. Everyone connected with the team felt that way.

Consequently, when the new season began with so much optimism, the six-game losing streak at the the genesis of 1974 had everyone scratching their head.

That opener at Busch Stadium was really something. The Pirates battled back to take the lead over the Cards by the score of 5-4. Richie Hebner hit two big homers in that effort. Then came the home half of the ninth. The Cardinals loaded the bases and had Lou Brock coming up to the plate. Brock hit a smash to Gene Clines. He trapped the ball and whipped it to the infield, so it was actually a hit. But, in the confusion, the Buccos threw the ball to home for a forceout. Then Mike Ryan threw to Richie Hebner for another forceout at third. Hebner then relayed the ball to second to Stennett for a triple play. But the umpires, for some reason, only called two outs instead of three. Ted Sizemore, always the Pirate killer, then won the game with an rbi hit. After the game, umpire Ed Sudol said that if Taveras had been alert he should have stepped on second and they would have had a triple play. The amazing thing about that was that Taveras was not even in the play. Umpire Satch Davidson, the second base umpire, declared that Stennett did not touch the bag, or if he did, I didn't see him. Another umpire opined,"The Pirates had a lot of gaul to expect a triple play on a single by Brock." After analyzing the situation, two more problems emerged. Earlier in the inning, Bake McBride bunted the ball out of the box, which is an automatic out. Aslo, in an irony of ironies, Brock overran a runner on that confusing triple play that became a double play, which is another automatic out. So the Pirates got six outs but were only credited with two and that cost them the game in the bottom of the ninth.

The second contest had no controversy at all as Cardinal Sonny Siebert shutout the Buccos and Bob Moose to the tune of 8-0. Evidently, Moose tired in the game and the

Cardinals took full advantage of that fact.

The two clubs couldn't play the third game on Sunday, April 7th, due to rain.

So the Pirates headed home for their April 9th opener with the Expos at Three Rivers Stadium.

As sometimes happens in Pittsburgh in April, the snow forced cancellation of the opener. It had been somewhat of a mild winter anyway. So the Pirates called off the game.

Everyone went home to watch the game between the Braves and the Dodgers. Hank Aaron hit number 715 that night against Al Downing and the Dodgers.

The Pirates and Expos gave the fans a real show on April 10th with an extra-inning affair. Initially, the Expos took a 5-1 lead. Then the Buccos took the lead in their next at bat by a 6-5 count. In the ninth, Bob Robertson slammed a two-run homer to send the game into extra innings. Eventually, the Pirates lost by a score of 12-8 in 13 innings, as Ramon Hernandez got credited with the loss.

Steve Rogers defeated the Buccos and Dock Ellis by a 5-1 count in the next contest to drop the Pirates record to 0-4.

Then came a wild game on Good Friday Night as the Buccos lost 7-6. It looked good in the early going with Dave Parker getting a three-run homer to put the Pirates up 4-0. Then the Cardinals scored six runs in the seventh to take the lead. The Buccos scored one in the eighth to make it 6-5. In the ninth, Willie Stargell lead off against Al Hrabosky. Wilver beat the "Stargell shift" by hitting the ball to third base. Somehow, however, Sizemore got the ball and threw him out at first. Richie Zisk then slammed a homer to right-center that tied the game at 6. In the eleventh, the Cardinals scored the winning run.

On Saturday, the Pirates lost 6-4, as Lynn McGlothen defeated Jim Rooker. The Pirates had the distinction of being the only team in major league baseball without a win!

Thankfully, on Easter Sunday, the Pirates experienced a rebirth of sorts with their first win in the first game of the doubleheader, 8-4, as Stennett continued with his hot bat, Parker slaughtered St Louis pitching once again and Stargell got his first roundtripper of the season. Bob Moose got credit for the Buccos first win of the new season. But in the nightcap, the Pirates lost 6-5 behind some shoddy defense. Bob Robertson played first base, Dal Maxvill saw time at shortstop and Dave Parker appeared in rightfield.

Now it was time to go on the road again, this time to Wrigley Field.

In the first game of the roadtrip on April 16th, pitcher Bruce Kison got credit for the 8-5 triumph that went twelve innings, after relieving Dock Ellis. After Frank Taveras singled, and another Bucco got on, Manny Sanguillen, playing in only his second game of the season, slammed a two run double that lead the way to victory. Richie Hebner picked up three hits in four at bats, including his third homer. Dave Parker raised his batting

Mario Mendoza   **#11**

average above .400 with a three for six performance.

The Cubs thoroughly throttled the Buccos to the tune of 18-9 the next day as Burt Hooton defeated Jerry Reuss. Things got so bad that Murtaugh stuck Steve Blass in there to at least get some work. But he still had his problems as he gave up eight runs, five hits and seven walks in five frames. The Cubs batted around against him in the fourth and he gave up back to back homers in the sixth. George Mitterwald, the Chicago catcher, double once and homered three times, including a grand slam, setting a club record of fourteen total bases while also driving in eight runs.

Cubs' pitcher Ken Frailing then hurled a 1-0 shutout against Pittsburgh the next day to outperform Jim Rooker. The Pirates actually lost due to an error.

In the next series, a two-game set in Shea Stadium, the Pirates hoped to break out of the funk. They lost to Jerry Koosman 5-2 on April 20th and then actually defeated Tom Seaver by a 7-0 count the next day. In the April 20th contest, the Buccos held a 2-0 lead before losing with the aid of a Gene Clines error as a ball off the bat of Bud Harrelson trickled out of his glove. In the triumph over the usually unhittable Tom Seaver, the Pirate bats jumped on "Tom Terrific" in the fourth inning by sending eight men to the plate en route to a 4-0 lead. Ken Brett picked up his first victory of the season by holding the Mets to three safeties.

After that 3-10 start, GM Joe L. Brown made more roster moves. Steve Blass, unable to get things together, headed down to the Charleston Charlies and Jim Sadowski replaced him on the roster. Dal Maxvill played less and less as the Pirates, reportedly due to an injury. Yet the Pirates felt more confident with Frank Taveras at short.

Mario Mendoza actually came up and took over the number 11 jersey from Maxvill after having only played two games of AAA ball, a happening that delighted the fans who witnessed his defensive wizardry. One writer actually declared that Mario handled ground balls with the same adeptness that Joe DiMaggio displayed with fly balls!

Little did Mario know that he would be famous for something far more dubious, that famous "Mendoza line," which is "the figurative boundary in the batting averages between those batters hitting above and below .215."(1) Reportedly, "the term was coined by Tom Paciorek or Bruce Bochte; broadcaster Mel Proctor said Mendoza, while playing for Seattle, was hitting above and below .200 and that teammates Paciorek and Bochte commented on that fact in an interview, and later Brett picked up on it and used the term."(quote from The New Dickson Baseball Dictionary, p. 322) In his nine seasons, Mario compiled a batting average of .215, five times finishing under .200.

Richie Hebner's hot start put him among the league's elite as he, Jimmy "Toy Canon" Wynn of the Astros and Tony Perez of the Reds stood tied for the NL lead in homers with six.

After splitting with the Braves in Atlanta and dropping to 4-11, the Pirates finally won their first series in Houston. They took two out of three from the Astros at Three Rivers, winning the bookend games by 4-3 and 7-3 margins while losing the middle game, 10-7. Ken Brett's win on April 28th raised the Pirate record to 6-12.

On May 1st, Dock Ellis hurled one of his most bizarre games in history as he hit the first three Reds' batters in the game, which set a major league record. He walked another batter before Murtaugh called for relief. Ellis claimed that he was high on pep pills at the time. Clay Carroll actually got the win in the Reds' 5-3 victory and the Pirates John Morlan took the loss.

Jerry Reuss picked up his first win of the season against the Braves on May 3rd in a 4-2 triumph.

Then came one of those famous bottom of the ninth inning victories on May 4th. The Buccos lead 2-0 in the early going. Then the Braves got to within one run. Hank Aaron came to the plate later in the game and suddenly Atlanta took a 3-2 lead. Then came the ninth. Pirate bats rallied for a 4-3 victory and the Buccos had an 8-13 mark.

On Sunday, May 5th, Ron Reed defeated the Pirates 3-2 at Three Rivers and the Buccos sank to 8-14.

The Buccos took a roadtrip to Houston and lost two out of three in the Astrodome. They lost the first two games by scores of 2-1 and 8-6, then rebounded behind Jim Rooker for a 4-1 victory on May 9th that put their record at 9-16.

Then came another four-game losing streak that plummeted the Pirates to a 9-20 record. The Buccos lost three consecutive to the Phillies at Veteran's Stadium by margins of 3-2, 2-1 and 8-6, as Dick Ruthven, Steve Carlton and Ed Farmer outhurled our triumvirate of Ken Brett, Bob Moose and Dock Ellis. The fourth consecutive loss came on May 14th at Three Rivers as Rick Reuschel defeated Jerry Reuss by a 7-1 count.

Bruce Kison and Ken Brett rallied the Buccos with back-to-back wins on May 15th and 16th against the Cubs, but then the Pirates fell back again.

Those pesky crosstate rivals, the Philadelphia Phillies, came to town and won two out of three against the Buccos. Ron Schueler won the Saturday game by a 9-2 score and then the two teams split a doubleheader on Sunday. Jim Lonborg defeated Dock Ellis 3-2 in the opener and then Jerry Reuss triumphed over Dick Ruthven in the nightcap.

Then came that roadtrip that everyone loves, the one north of the border to Parc Jarry in Montreal. Mike Torrez defeated Jim Rooker and the Pirates by a 4-2 score on May 20th. Then, on the 21st, Ken Brett won to the tune of 8-4 despite injuries to Rennie Stennett and Dave Parker while they circled the bases. After Steve Rogers triumphed over Bruce Kison on May 22nd by a 5-4 score, the Pirates dropped to a record of 13-24, eleven games under .500.

Strangely, catcher Mike Ryan fell down his basement steps at his home in Pittsburgh. Thank goodness it wasn't that serious. But people wondered if it could get any worse for the Buccos.

On Friday, May 24th, Pirate officials honored the straight A students of the Pittsburgh high schools with free tickets. Of the 12,000 fans in attendance, 4,000 were A students. All students with a grade point average of 3.6 or higher got the chance to get the tickets, a joint program sponsored by the Pirates and the Pittsburgh Press. The Pirates showed all those in attendance that they could make the grade with a 4-1 victory over the Mets, aided by two runs in the first frame that came as the result of two-baggers by Stargell and Zisk. It was an interesting matchup of quality NL lefthanders Jerry Reuss and John Matlack. Everyone in attendance hoped to see the Pirates get an A rating on their report card for the rest of the season. They had earned an F up to this point.

John Milner's homer helped the Mets triumph over the Pirates by a 4-3 count as Jerry Koosman defeated Dock Ellis.

Then, on May 26th, the Mets defeated the Pirates by a 5-3 margin, which dropped Pittsburgh to a 14-26 mark. Ray Sadecki defeated Dave Giusti.

Three Rivers Stadium hosted a Memorial Day doubleheader between the Pirates and the Padres on Monday, May 27th, one of the most memorable twinbills ever for Ken Brett. In the opener, Ken Brett hurled a masterful ballgame, holding the Padres without a hit until Fred Kendall, whose son would later catch for the Buccos, broke it up in the ninth frame with a groundball single to leftfield. He ended up with a two-hit 6-0 shutout as Thomas' two-out double was the only other safety. Then, in the nightcap, Ken Brett tripled, as a pinchhitter, in two runs to help the Buccos win 8-7. How many pitchers can ever top that, nearly pitching a no-hitter and then getting the game-winning pinchhit triple? That had to be his greatest day in baseball! Richie Hebner slammed his eighth homer in the second game and Richie Zisk clubbed his fourth homer in the first contest.

Jerry Reuss hurled the Buccos to their third straight win with a magnificent five-hitter on May 29th in a 13-3 slugfest against the Padres at Three Rivers. Bob Robertson, the big readhead whom many had proclaimed "Pittsburgh's next Kiner," accounted for five rbi with two roundtrippers and a single. It seemed that Reuss and Robertson looked like they

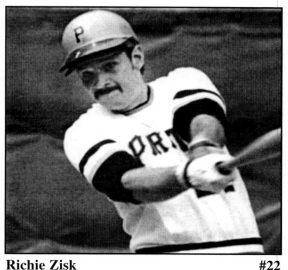

Richie Zisk   **#22**

were ready to rally.

Then, on the last day of the month, the Pirates lost to the Reds and Pedro Borbon by a 7-5 score to end up with a record of 17-27. Johnny Bench slugged a triple with the bases loaded in the seventh inning to rally the Reds from a 5-0 deficit. Bob Robertson clubbed two more homers and picked up three more rbi.

They posted an 11-15 record for the month of May.

June 1st started with a bang for the Pirates in their 14-1 triumph over their rivals, the Cincinnati Reds. They knocked out eighteen hits in an awesome display of power. Hebner, Robertson and Zisk all clubbed circuit clouts. Richie Zisk collected three rbi while four batters, Hebner, Oliver, Stargell and Robertson, had two rbi. Other extra-base hits included a triple by Frank Taveras, two doubles by Willie Stargell and one double each by Brett, Oliver and Sanguillen.

Consequently, after Ken Brett's marvelous showing, he got Player of the Week honors in the National League for the week of May27th-June 2nd. Trading away Dave Cash over the winter now didn't seem so bad. It would look even better when Dave Cash and Ken Brett would both make the NL All-Star team.

Joe L. Brown's moves continued. He brought up Larry Demery from Charleston and that turned out to be a wonderful move as he hurled many fine innings for the squad. Scouting reports on him classified him as someone who possessed one of the better arms in the organization with a good fastball, good curve and a good change up. Although he lacked consistency and control, Brown thought him a worthy addition to the roster.

On June 2nd, the Pirates lost to Fred Norman and the Reds by a count of 5-1 and immediately went into another tailspin.

Dodger Stadium again proved unfriendly to the Pirates, more for the Los Angeles pitching than the actual atmosphere of Chavez Ravine. The Buccos lost three straight to the Dodgers, whom they would face in the NLCS in October. Two of the Dodgers pitchers actually whitewashed the Pirates, Tommy John by a 5-0 mark on the 4th and Andy Messersmith by a 6-0 mark on the 6th. Coupled with a 3-2 loss to Mike Marshall and you had a sweep that left the Buccos with a record of 18-31.

Larry Demery got his first action on June 7th at Candlestick Park and John D'Acquisto defeated him and the Buccos 6-2 to drop the Pirates fourteen games under .500 at 18-32. D'Acquisto hit his first major league homer. Rookie righthander Larry Demery started the game and yielded five runs in four innings.

Fortunately, the Pirates took the last two games of the series at Candlestick. Dock Ellis defeated the Giants 5-2 on June 8th. Then Jerry Reuss enjoyed another blowout, this time by a 14-1 margin, on the 9th. Richie Zisk further displayed his hitting prowess as he hit for the cycle in that slugfest, hitting a three-run homer in the first, doubling in the fifth, singling in the sixth and tripling in the ninth. Bob Robertson doubled and homered while Stargell also had a big night.

Richie Zisk's development thrilled the Pirates as he at least provided power and rbi that the team desperately needed with the death of Clemente and the general malaise of the Pirate bats in 1973. Although fans often lost sight of him in the midst of Stargell, Parker, and Oliver, he still stood as one of the key components of The Lumber Company. His .321 batting average up to this point showed that his .324 mark in '73 was no fluke.

Team members point to June 10th as perhaps the most depressing night of the season as the Pirates dropped a 9-8 decision to the Padres after leading 8-1 going into the last two frames. Jim Rooker lost his composure after the game as he declared,"I want out. I've had it. I couldn't care less about things here right now. I think I deserve the right to win or lose the game myself. Our bullpen has been terrible. I wouldn't say it if it wasn't true." Two weeks earlier he had also aired his grievances in much the same way. Kent Tekulve lost the game in relief.

To understand the frustration, you could just look at the stats. Statistics don't always tell the story but in this case they did. Richie Zisk stood as the only hitter above .300 while Hebner stood 4 points below that standard. Oliver and Stargell struggled to get to .280 and other players, such as Sanguillen, also stood well below their career averages. Pitching also stunk as the Pirates team era reached 4.10, which meant that only two teams, Chicago and San Diego, had poorer pitching staffs.

Many observers thought that the Pirates simply had to change their usual style, from their free-swinging ways to a more fundamental approach, and they could not do that.

Others pointed to the losses of Roberto Clemente and Steve Blass as the two big reasons for the collapse.

The Pirates split a pair of 5-2 scores with the Padres, as Ken Brett beat Randy Jones on June 11th and Dave Freisleben defeated Larry Demery on the 12th. That left the Buccos with a 21-34 mark as they prepared to return to Three Rivers.

That return meant a great deal to the team.

San Francisco's Giants came to town for a three-game series and the Pirates swept them by scores of 4-2, 3-2 and 4-3 as Dock Ellis, Daryl Patterson and Jim Rooker all picked up victories. This modest three-game streak got the momentum going.

Next came the Dodgers. Ken Brett defeated Don Sutton 7-3 in the first contest and then Dave Giusti triumphed over Tommy John in a 2-0 whitewashing. Jerry Reuss then raised his record to 6-4 with a 7-3 victory for the Buccos sixth straight victory, which meant that they won every game in their homestand and improved their record to 27-34.

In that sixth straight victory, fans witnessed a bit of bizarre baseball history. At one point in the game, Joe Ferguson struck out with the bases loaded and walked away. Manny Sanguillen then rolled the ball to the mound, apparently unaware that the Pirates had not yet retired the side. Lee Lacy, who had been on third, jogged to the dugout. Jimmy Wynn, the runner who had been on second base, came around to score but Sanguillen tagged him out. Lacy noticed what had happened and hurredly raced to the plate and got tagged out. According to the rules, the umpires ruled Lacy safe despite being tagged out. Fortunately, that crazy play had nothing to do with the outcome of the game.

The Pirate Ship cruised into Chicago's Wrigley Field for a four-game series and the Cubs took three out of four to put Pittsburgh back into the hole again. Rick Reuschel whitewashed the Pirates by a 3-0 margin and then the Cubs' Steve Stone won a 3-2 decision the next day. Ken Brett raised his record to 9-4 with a 6-0 shutout of the Cubs on June 22nd. Then the Pirates lost to Bill Bonham and the Cubs on June 23rd by a 7-3 count. As if things weren't already horrible enough, the Pirates asked for a Chicago police escort out of Wrigley because authorities received four death threats against Frank Taveras.

Busch Stadium provided the venue for the next four games and the Cardinals took three out of four to drop the Pirates to 29-40. The Pirates lost a doubleheader to the Cardinals on the 24th by 3-1 and 4-0 scores, the latter a shutout by Bob Gibson. Al Hrabosky won an 8-7 decision on the 25th. But the Pirates prevented the sweep with a 7-2 victory on the 26th as Jim Rooker defeated Sonny Siebert and Stargell had a three-run blast.

Pittsburgh came back home after that disastrous 2-6 roadtrip ready for the second-place Philadelphia Phillies.

The Buccos triumphed over Jim Lonborg, who had won his previous six decisions, by a 6-3 count as Zisk had the big blow with a bases-loaded two-bagger.

On June 30th, the Pirates returned to their big success- the doubleheader sweep. The Pirates' Ken Brett won his tenth game as he defeated former teammate Steve Carlton in the first game and eventually won 11-8, despite giving up seven tallies to the Phillies in the ninth inning. Richie Hebner clubbed his eleventh four-bagger of the season in the opener. In the nightcap, the Phillies went ahead 2-0 in the sixth inning on a double by Willie Montanez. The Pirate bats responded in the eighth with three consecutive extra-base hits, which themselves could be considered consecutive, a double by Oliver, a triple by Parker and then a homer by Zisk, his eighth of the campaign.

After taking two from the Expos, by 4-2 and 2-1 margins, the six-game winning streak raised the Pirate record to 34-40, only six games under .500. That sure looked better than being fourteen games under .500.

The Buccos closed out the homestand by splitting a July 4th doubleheader with Montreal, losing the opener to Steve Rogers by a 2-1 count and then winning the nightcap, 3-2.

Somehow, the Pirates dropped two out of three to the Astros in Houston and their record dropped to 36-43. Larry Dierker won 7-1 against Dock Ellis on the 5th and then Don Wilson whitewashed the Buccos 1-0 on the 6th. The Pirates defeated the Astros 6-4 to keep their head above water.

During this time, Pirate management realized that Kurt Bevacqua, obtained in a trade from Kansas City in December of 1973, had to go. "Dirty Kurt" had a reputation as a practical joker, court jester, cheerleader, opposition baiter, bench jockey, mimic and all-around good humor man. But his humor disappeared when he didn't play. The previous season, his first full season as a regular, he hit a respectable .257. So Joe L. Brown traded him right back to Kansas City on July 8th and received minor leaguer Cal Meier and cash in the deal.

That gave them another chance to make a move with an eleven-game homestand. But the home cooking didn't seem to help.

The Buccos dropped two out of three to the Atlanta Braves, beginning with a 5-0 shutout. After that, the Pirates defeated the Braves 5-4 and then lost 10-5. Fortunately, Ken Brett won his eleventh game for the Pirates in that middle game of the series. In that Pirate victory, the Buccos had to come from behind as the Braves led 2-0. The Pirates scored four runs in the next inning. Mario Mendoza scored the only other tally as he singled, went to third on Brett's single and scored on a fumble of Garr's throw by Perez.

On July 11th, the offday between the Braves' and Reds' series, Joe L. Brown acquired Chuck Brinkman from the Chicago

Art Howe   #14

White Sox for cash to replace the injured Mike Ryan.

General Manager Brown also brought up Art Howe from Charleston to help with the "hot corner" chores because of the injuries to Richie Hebner.

The Pirates chief rival of the '70's then came to Three Rivers for a five-game series. Cincinnati won four out of those five games and the Buccos dropped to 38-49, eleven games below .500.

In the first doubleheader of the series, Don Gullett hurled a five-hit 7-0 shutout in the opener and then Clay Carroll triumphed in the nightcap by a 4-3 margin.

The next day came a 9-4 triumph by Tom Hall over Jerry Reuss.

Many people expected a sweep after Fred Norman defeated Ken Brett 3-2 in the opener of the second doubleheader of the series.

Then came the nightcap. What a nightcap that was! Most people associated with the team believe that the fight in the nightcap turned the whole season around for the Pirates. It all started with Jack Billingham hitting Bruce Kison with a pitch in the fourth inning. Both teams came out onto the field after that. Reds' Manager Sparky Anderson accidentally stepped on Ed Kirkpatrick's foot. Kirkpatrick then shoved the Red's manager and Andy Kosko, a Cincinnati player, punched Ed. Sparky Anderson got mad at Mario Mendoza for taking a blind punch at Bill Plummer. Pedro Borbon then pinned Daryl Patterson and pulled some of his hair out and a portion of flesh. For some reason, that seemed to unite the Buccos. They went on a big winning streak immediately.

First, the Houston Astros came to town. The Pirates swept them

Dock Ellis pitched a beautiful game as he picked up his fourth victory. The Astros managed only one run on eight hits. Pittsburgh went ahead of the Astros, 2-1, in the fourth, as Oliver, Zisk, Sanguillen, Hebner and Taveras all singled. Taveras got another run in the seventh on a bunt hit, a sacrifice, a groundout and, finally, an error by Tommy Helms on a groundball off of the bat of Gene Clines.

Jim Rooker defeated Larry Dierker in the next game by a 6-2 mark.

Then, on the 17th, Larry Demery got his first major league victory and also his first big league hit. The Bucco bats made it easy with seventeen hits and eleven runs. Demery went 7 2/3 innings and then left in favor of Ramon Hernandez in this 11-3 triumph over Houston. The two Richies again lead the way as Zisk went three for four with four rbi and Hebner had four safeties. Larry Demery had a triple as his first major league safety.

Jerry Reuss shutout Ron Reed and the Braves 4-0 on July 18th for the team's fifth straight victory.

On July 19th, Ken Brett again showed his incredible all-around ability as he hurled a 2-0 shutout against the Braves' Phil Niekro for his 12th victory and also helped himself with the bat. Brett drove Frank Taveras home with the first run of the contest with a sacrifice fly after the Dominican shortstop had tripled. The other run came with two out in the top of the ninth as "Spanky" Kirkpatrick drew a walk and then Bob Robertson drove him home with a pinchit double.

On Saturday, July 20th, the Buccos won their seventh straight game with a 7-6 triumph over the Braves. Wilver Stargell hit the game-winning homer in the eleventh inning. For all of those baseball historians out there, Hank Aaron played in his 3,034th game, breaking Ty Cobb's record.

Dock Ellis won his fifth game and sent the Pirates into the all-star break with a mighty positive disposition with their eighth consecutive victory in a 6-2 triumph over Buzz Capra and the Braves. The Pirates went into the all-star break with a much-improved 45-49 mark and stood in fourth place, only 3.5 games out of first.

That got everyone fired up for the 45th All-Star Game since it would take place at Three Rivers Stadium on July 23rd. Sixteen future Hall-of-Famers would appear in this game.

Interestingly enough, Yogi Berra picked Ken Brett from the Pirates as the team's representative. It was also quite interesting that former Pirate Dave Cash appeared in the game.

The National League won the game by a score of 7-2. Reggie Smith hit a homer and Brett was the winning pitcher! Kenny pitched two masterful innings, allowing no runs to score. Steve Garvey, who picked up a single and a double and also made a

Ken Brett   **#30**

spectacular play in the field, won the MVP Award.

Yogi Berra got the boos from the hometown fans during the pre-game introductions because he had only picked one Pirate representative.

Dave Cash, a former Pirate, had the final assist of the game to Steve Garvey!

It was great to see the different stars from the National League and American League get together for a meaningful all-star encounter with Tiant, Perry, Jackson, Rudi, Campaneris and Allen, among many, many others.

The Pirates opened the second half of the season with a doubleheader against the Montreal Expos in Parc Jarry on July 25th. Steve Renko defeated Jim Rooker in the opener by a 10-5 margin. In the nightcap, the Expos sent another Steve to the mound, Steve Rogers, and Jerry Reuss got his tenth win of the campaign, 3-2. Sanguillen and Stargell both hit homers in that second game. Rookie Art Howe, recently recalled from Charleston, then scored the decisive run when he tripled in the eighth and then came home on an Al Oliver single. It was a much-needed insurance run as Montreal notched one run in the ninth and Giusti had to shut them down. Al Oliver extended his hitting streak to 21 games with a homer in the first game and a single in the second.

Dock Ellis and Ramon Hernandez then combined to whitewash the Expos by a 3-0 count on July 26th. Dock improved his record to 6-8 with his third straight victory. Al Oliver hit safely in his 22nd consecutive game. The Buccos had won ten of their last eleven.

Then the Phillies swept the Buccos by scores of 7-4 and 6-5 behind the hurling of Pete Richert and Wayne Twitchell at Veteran's Stadium on the 27th. Amazingly, both teams stranded eighteen men on the basepaths in the doubledip. Ken Brett and Bruce Kison took the losses.

On Sunday, July 28th, the Pirates played their brand of comeback baseball as they defeated the Phillies, 4-3. That brought the Buccos within four games of first place and also four away from the .500 mark.

Yet the final contest of the Phillies series ended with a 13-1 blowout as Steve Carlton outhurled our lefthanded ace Jerry Reuss.

It was time to go to Shea Stadium for a series with the New York Mets.

In another of those doubleheaders, Jim Rooker shutout Jon Matlack, 6-0. Jerry Koosman then salvaged the second game for New York with a 4-3 triumph.

That meant the Buccos would face Tom Seaver again on the final day of July and the Pirate bats slammed twelve hits in 4 1/3 frames against him. In the first frame, Seaver retired the first two batters. Two-out lightning took its toll, however, as Oliver tripled and Stargell followed with his 18th homer. Everyone hit safely in the game. Dock Ellis even drove in Ed Kirkpatrick with a single in the fifth. The Buccos prevailed, 8-3.

The Pirates had a record of 13-9 for the month of July in improving their record to 50-54.

Dave Giusti lost the August 1st contest against the Cardinals at Three Rivers in the eleventh inning as the Pirates went into the frame tied 2-2 and lost, 5-2.

The Buccos didn't let that bother them though as they came back the next night with a 3-2 extra-inning victory. Richie Hebner singled to score Ed Kirkpatrick with the winning tally in the bottom of the 14th and Ramon Hernandez picked up the win in relief against St Louis' Orlando Pena.

Chicago came to town and won two out of three. Rick Reuschel won the opener on August 3rd, 4-3. Then Bill Bonham followed that with a 4-3 triumph the next day in the first game of the doubleheader. Bruce Kison saved the day for the Pirates with a 7-1 triumph in the final contest.

Then the Mets came to Three Rivers and the Pirates started another impressive winning streak.

On August 6th, the Pirates won another extra-inning game to the musical tune of 9-8 as they benefited from two Met errors in the bottom of the eleventh frame. Daryl Patterson defeated Tug McGraw, who went down with Lee Smith as the most snake-bitten opposing relief pitcher in Three Rivers history!

Larry Demery gained his second straight victory the next night with a three-hit 10-1 win.

Jerry Reuss won his eleventh game by a 4-3 mark against the Mets the next day and the Pirate win streak reached four games as the Pirate record improved to 55-57.

San Diego arrived in town for a three-game set and the Pirates won two out of three from the Padres. Jim Rooker lead the Buccos to their fifth consecutive victory and got them to within one game of the .500 mark with a triumph over Randy Jones. After John Morlan endured an 8-4 loss on the 10th, Dock Ellis came back to even his season record at 8-8 with an 8-1 triumph.

The Pirates went on the road for a critical series at Riverfront and Jerry Reuss won his twelfth game of the campaign with a 7-4 win as the Pirates got back to the .500 level at 58-58. Dave Giusti got the save. Willie Stargell and Ed Kirkpatrick both clubbed two-run first inning homers to stake the Buccos to a 5-0 lead. Then the Pirates held on for the victory.

Inspired after reaching the .500 mark, the Buccos responded with their highest hit total of the season with 21 safeties in a 14-3 thrashing of Cincinnati as Larry Demery bested Jack Billingham. Al Oliver drove in five runs and picked up his eighth homer. Ed Kirkpatrick hit another roundtripper and had two rbi. Richie Zisk had three rbi. The Pirates scored at least two runs against each Reds' hurler.

In the final game of the series, Cincinnati avoided a sweep with a 3-2 tenth-inning victory. Cesar Geronimo doubled against Ramon Hernandez in the bottom of the tenth to score Dave Concepcion with the game-winning run. How's that for a latin connection! Richie Zisk narrowly missed one of baseball's great records in that last game against the Reds. He failed by one game to equal Mel Ott's NL record of picking up an rbi in eleven straight contests. Zisk drove in thirteen runs during the ten-game streak. The major league record stands at twelve games, accomplished by Hall-of-

Famers Joe Cronin and Ted Williams.

Dock Ellis defeated Don Sutton on August 16th in the Buccos return to Three Rivers to put Pittsburgh one game over .500 again.

Then, on August 17th, Dave Giusti relieved in the ninth with runners on the corners and one out. Anything other than a strikeout or a double play would score the tying run from third base. Buckner hit a slow roller to shorstop Frank Taveras. The Pirate shortstop shoveled the ball to Stennett whose relay to first nipped Buckner by a half a step. A relief pitcher couldn't script it any better than that. The Buccos were two games over .500 and only 2.5 games out of first.

The Pirates completed the sweep on August 18th with a 10-3 win as Larry Demery evened his record at 4-4 in defeating Geoff Zahn. The Buccos stood at 62-59.

Appropriately, Richie Zisk and Al Oliver tied for Player of the Week honors in the NL from August 12-18. Zisk batted .448 with thirteen hits, which included a triple, a homer and four doubles in twenty-nine at bats, also barely missing the consecutive rbi/game streak. Oliver collected thirteen safeties with two doubles and a homer in twenty-eight at bats. Al scored seven runs, drove in eight and sported a .464 average. Oliver also had a thirteen-game batting streak and had hit safely in 49 of his last 53 contests.

Ken Brett complained about his elbow problems, a malady that came about as a result of his two innings of work in the All-Star Game. He admitted,"I got out of my personal routine because of that game. When I got into the game, I was all tensed up and I think I overthrew the ball. I couldn't throw a ball 25 feet right now."

The Giants came to town for a three-game series and beat the Pirates two out of three. They won by scores of 5-3 and 8-7 in the first two games of the series. Fortunately, the Cardinals also lost those nights. So the Pirates won the final game as Dock Ellis defeated Ed Halicki by a 4-2 count and the Buccos actually got within 1.5 games of the top.

Jerry Reuss got the roadtrip off to a good start against San Diego in Jack Murphy Stadium with a 6-2 victory on August 23rd to improve his record to 14-9. That also improved the Bucco record to 64-61. Manny Sanguillen went three for five at the plate. Richie Zisk picked up three hits in four at bats. Rennie Stennett and Al Oliver both added two safeties.

The Pirates and Padres had a scheduled game the next day. Somehow, in a weird twist of events, Jack Murphy Stadium officials had erred by scheduling the Chargers and the Padres for a game the same day. The Chargers got the nod so that forced a doubleheader on Sunday.

That day off gave Willie Stargell time to worry about the imminent publication of his new book entitled, OUT OF LEFT FIELD. The Pirate slugger revealed that the intimate conversations and activities involving himself and his teammates embarrassed him. Approximately 100 advance copies went out to reviewers before the tentative publication date of August 26th.   Some people affirmed that the book might damage Stargell's reputation because of its controversial material. The publisher lead Stargell to believe that the book would deal with his personal life in a way that would be palatable to children. But that wasn't the case as one newspaper reported,"Stargell's objection to the content stems from the candid conversations about sex and drugs." Publisher Little Brown and Company recalled the book.

Joe L. Brown kept up his wheeling and dealing to improve the club for the stretch run by purchasing the contract of Puerto Rican pitcher Juan Pizarro from the Cordoba team in the Mexican League. Two main reasons made this acquisition critical- the injury to Ken Brett and Pizarro's versatility as a spot starter, long reliever or short man. He would wear number 49 and Darryl Patterson would return to Charleston to make room on the roster. Juan sported a 13-6 record with Cordoba, which included nine shutouts, five in a row, and an era of 1.57. This stood as Pizarro's second stint with the Buccos, having also hurled for Pittsburgh in '67-'68.

Then came the horrible news that reverberated through the whole organization. Alfredo Edmead, a very talented minor league outfielder with the Salem, Virginia, Pirates, died as a result of a freak play. Rocky Mount N.C. hurler Murray Gage-Cole lofted a short fly to rightfield. Salem second sacker Pablo Cruz drifted back to field it as Edmead came charging in like a race horse. Cruz caught the ball and Alfredo Edmead dove. Alfredo's head hit Pablo's knee and he crumpled on the field in a pool of blood. On the way to the hospital, he died of a massive skull fracture. It became the first fatality in organized baseball since Cleveland's Ray Chapman died from a Carl Mays' beaning in 1920.

People in the Pirate organization lamented the death of the 18-year-old Edmead because he had his whole life in front of him, as people inevitably say. Only the day before, he made the Class A Carolina League All-Star team because he compiled statistics in his first full season that included a .319 batting average with 7 homers, 59 rbi and 59 stolen bases. Some considered him a Clemente prototype.

Salem manager Johnny Lipon admitted,"Edmead was such a spark of life. We all lost a little bit of our lives with him."

Perhaps the most ironic thing was that Pablo Cruz was Edmead's best friend.

So, after all this food for thought filled up the Pirates craniums, it was time to get back to baseball.

In that doubleheader, the Buccos again got the brooms out. They won both games by scores of 4-1 and 10-2. In the initial contest, the Pirates scored three times in the twelfth inning on only one hit to get the win. Two of the runs scored on walks and the other came across the plate on a sacrifice fly by Richie Zisk. In the nightcap, the Buccos fought back from a 2-1 deficit with three runs in the seventh. Six more runs in the ninth turned it into a rout. Jim Rooker won the first game and Larry Demery raised his record to 5-4 in the nightcap. The sweep propelled the Pirates into first place and raised their record to 66-61.

Now it was time to go to San Francisco's Candlestick Park.

The Pirates throttled the Giants 13-2 on August 27th as Dock Ellis defeated John D'Acquisto and improved his record to 11-8. Dock, one of the better hitting pitchers, even had two rbi on his hit as he won his eighth straight. In the Pirates big inning, Al Oliver had two doubles and four rbi. In that inning, when fourteen batters came to the plate, the Pirate picked up five walks, two hit batsmen, an error and also the hits. Oliver picked up another rbi with a single in the ninth. For the night, Oliver had three hits in five at bats and five rbi.

In the eleventh inning at Candlestick the next night, Ed Kirkpatrick got another clutch hit in the eleventh frame to defeat the Giants, 3-1, for the Buccos sixth straight win. They now stood at 68-61.

Dave Kingman homered in the bottom of the eleventh against Dave Giusti to defeat the Pirates by a 3-2 count the next night.

Pittsburgh closed out the month with two straight 4-3 triumphs over the Dodgers at Dodger Stadium to raise their record to 70-62 as Jim Rooker and Larry Demery got the wins and Dave Giusti picked up two saves. Jim Rooker got back to .500 and the Pirates actually scored against Mike Marshall in the first game. In the second 4-3 victory, the Buccos exploded for four runs in the sixth inning aided by a Richie Zisk homer. That was Larry Demery's sixth straight win, quite an accomplishment after his 0-4 start.

The Pirates lost to the Dodgers on September 1st by a 6-2 count but still managed to have a 7-2 record on the roadtrip. For the month of August, they sported a 20-9 record and were the hottest team in baseball.

So the Buccos truly enjoyed their traditional Labor Day doubleheader on Monday, September 2nd, as they continued with their hot streak. They swept their crossstate rivals by scores of 7-4 and 11-1 to raise their record to 72-63. About 50,000 fans showed up for that double dip.

In the first game, the Pirates defeated Steve Carlton, after trailing, 3-1. In a strange type of delay, the umpires allowed a 16-minute pause while Carlton requested that the ground crew fix up the pitcher's mound. Many thought the game was over because of Steve Carlton's dominant pitching style. Yet Willie Stargell clubbed a key homer to cut the lead to 3-2. Later in the contest, Stargell singled and Bob Robertson homered to give the Pirates a 6-4 lead amid thunderous applause. Willie Stargell then slammed another homer in the seventh to make the final 7-4 and give Jerry Reuss a 15-9 record.

The nightcap proved to be no contest as Bruce Kison evened his record at 7-7 as the Pirates thrashed the Phillies by a 11-1 score. Kison irritated former Pirate Dave Cash when he threw at him during the contest, declaring "there was not excuse for that." Bruce replied that only a jerk would throw at someone in a blowout situation like that.

Jim Rooker won his eleventh game the next day as the Pirates completed their sweep of the Phillies with an 8-2 victory.

Dave Parker   **#39**

Montreal then came to town for a series on September 6th, 7th and 8th and the Pirates swept them by scores of 2-1, 6-5 and 8-2. In the 2-1 victory, Ed Kirkpatrick again got a big hit as he slammed a homer for the winning margin, truly showing Brown's trading for him was a wise move.

Dave Parker came through with an important single in the twelfth inning in the second win as the Pirates maintained their 1.5 game lead on the Cardinals, who also won. In the third contest, Jim Rooker defeated Steve Rogers for his twelfth victory and the Pirates improved their record to 76-63.

The Buccos went on a roadtrip that started in Wrigley Field and split the two games there. In the first contest, Steve Stone defeated Larry Demery by a count of 9-4 as the Cubs' power hitting dominated the contest. On September 10th, Ken Brett made his comeback after his injury and defeated the Cubs, 12-4. That same night, as Lou Brock stole his 104th and 105th bases, the Cardinals lost to the Phillies, 8-2. That put the Pirates 3.5 games ahead of St Louis.

Then came the disastrous six-game losing streak that plummeted the Pirates into second place.

On September 11th, the Phillies' Willie Montanez' line drive hit Dock Ellis as the Pirates held a 4-1 lead in the sixth. That changed the momentum of the game and the Pirates lost 8-5 as Ramon Hernandez got the loss. But, more importantly, the Pirates lost Dock Ellis for the rest of the season.

The next night, the Pirates held a 4-0 lead with Jerry Reuss on the hill. Then, inexplicably, the Phillies scored six runs in the eighth inning and won the game, 6-4.

Montreal's Expos then returned the favor to the Pirates by sweeping them in Parc Jarry by scores of 3-2, 17-2 and 5-4 as Jim Rooker, Larry Demery and Ken Brett went down to defeat. In the middle game of the series, the 17-2 blowout, the Pirates dropped out of first place by a half a game.

The next night, the Pirates hosted the St Louis Cardinals in the first-game of a critical series that would help decide the division. In a dramatic 13-inning affair, the Cardinals won 2-1 as Lou Brock scored the deciding run on a sacrifice fly. That win meant that the Pirates had now lost six straight and the Cardinals had won six consecutive to move Pittsburgh from 3.5 games in front to 2.5 lengths behind St Louis. The division race had completely changed in a week.

The Pirates ended their losing streak the next night with a 4-1 win behind the hurling of Jim Rooker.

Then the Pirates got another clutch 8-6 win versus Al Hrabosky and the Cardinals the next night. After trailing by a 4-3 margin, the Pirate bats exploded for five runs against the normally unhittable Al Hrabosky, which included a key three-run homer by Richie Hebner. The top of the ninth got a little scary. But Dave Giusti struck out the side to insure the triumph and picked up his eleventh save. So the Buccos got back to within a half a game of the Cardinals.

New York came to town September 20th and the Buccos defeated Tug McGraw in the bottom of the ninth by a score of 4-3. The Pirates scored three times in their last at bat. Rennie Stennett crossed the plate with the winning tally as John Milner tried for a double play instead of trying to get the sprinting Stennett at home. The standings stayed the same as the Cardinals also won.

The Pirates then lost the last two games of the series to the Mets to drop 1.5 games out of first again. Jerry Koosman defeated Juan Pizarro, whom the Pirates acquired from the Mexican League, by a 4-2 margin in the first one. Jon Matlack then whitewashed Jerry Reuss 4-0 in the next contest.

September 23rd then became another key matchup between the Cardinals and Pirates, this time at Busch Stadium. Jim Rooker and Lynn McGlothen both hurled ten innings. Richie Hebner got the winning hit with an rbi single up the middle that scored Miguel Dilone. Manny Sanguillen gunned Lou Brock down at third base when he attempted to steal late in the game, a key play because Ted Sizemore followed that with a single on the next pitch. Rooker got his 14th victory and Giusti his 12th save. That got the Pirates back to within a half a game.

Jim Rooker   **#19**

The last nine games of the season would decide everything, two more at Busch Stadium against St Louis, four with the Mets at Shea and then three against the Cubs at Three Rivers. Pittsburgh had lost nine of their last thirteen and badly needed a winning streak.

Pittsburgh responded to the pressure by defeating the Cardinals 7-3 the next night to get into a first-place tie. Bruce Kison evened his record at 8-8. In the first inning, it looked like the Cardinals would win as Lou Brock lead off the game with a single and Ted Sizemore drove him home. But Bruce got out of that threat with minimal damage. Dave Parker continued his onslaught against Cardinal pitching with a two-run single. Willie Stargell greeted hurler Rich Folkers with a three-run roundtripper. Rennie Stennett also had three hits.

In the third game of the series, the Pirates lost 13-12 in a wild affair. In the early going, the Buccos lead by a 5-0 margin behind a three-run homer by Manny Sanguillen. Then the Cards tied it with some key hits past Richie Hebner at the "hot corner." They then went ahead on another hit. Then Al Oliver tied the game with a clutch extra-base hit. St Louis got three more, which included a homer by Ken Reitz. Then the Buccos tied the game again. Everyone in Pittsburgh celebrated as the Pirates got three more runs to take the lead once again. The Cardinals, however, followed that up with four runs of their own and won the game. The Buccos trailed again by a half a game.

Juan Pizarro outdueled Jerry Koosman the next night by an 11-5 count at Shea Stadium as the Pirates moved back into a first-place tie with the Cardinals. Joe L. Brown's move to pick up Pizarro also looked very good this night. Al Oliver went five for five, including two homers, a double and two singles, to raise his batting average to .320, second only to Ralph Garr.

In another all-lefty matchup the following game, Jerry Reuss defeated Jon Matlack by a 2-1 count for his 16th victory. Reuss hurled a perfect game for the first four innings. When he got into trouble later in the game, his defense picked him up with key double plays. St Louis won again so the Pirates and Cards had identical 84-73 records.

Jim Rooker won his 15th game by a 7-3 count the following day, defeating Tug

McGraw. The two Richies, Zisk and Hebner, both unloaded big homers. Rennie Stennet and Al Oliver both continued their assault on the 200-hit mark. Rennie Stennett went 4 for 5 for the game and ended the day with 194 safeties. Al finished the day with 192 hits. Fans switched their televisions to watch the game between the Cards and Cubs that ended with Chicago prevailing 8-3, as Joe Torre, Mike Tyson and Al Hrabosky all made key errors and Billy Williams hit a homer. The Buccos lead by one game with four to play and now had a magic number-four!

On September 29th, the Mets' Bob Apodaca defeated Ken Brett by a 7-2 mark and the Pirates now had an 85-74 record.

Now the Cubs came to town for the crucial three-game series to end the season.

That first game saw Bruce Kison defeat Bill Bonham by a 2-1 count to improve the Pirates' record to 86-74. St Louis defeated the Expos and sported an identical record with two games to play.

On October 1st, the fans at Three Rivers erupted with cheers when the scoreboard operator flashed the following: Mike Jorgensen hit a homer in the bottom of the eighth inning and the Expos defeated the Cards. If the Pirates won, they would clinch a tie for the divisional title.

That happiness dissipated when the Cubs scored three times to take a 5-3 lead. The fans and players certainly didn't want another tie! Bob Robertson then clubbed one of the most dramatic pinchhit homeruns in Three Rivers history over the leftfield fence in the bottom of the eighth frame to give the Pirates a 6-5 triumph. Willie Stargell made a big play earlier by nailing Burris at the plate with a strong throw. Otherwise, Robertson's homer would only have tied the game. Pandemonium reigned in Pittsburgh. The Pirates lead by one game with one to play. Dave Giusti got the win and Dave LaRoche the loss.

Bob Robertson #7

It all came down to game 162! That's what baseball should be about. Before the game on October 2, the Pirates found out that rain postponed the game between the Cards and the Expos. They would play on thursday only if the Pirates lost. If the Pirates lost and the Cards won on thursday, the two teams would meet in a one-game playoff on friday to determine who would go to the NLCS.

So the Pirates wanted to eliminate any of those possibilities.

Game 162 went down to the bottom of the ninth with two outs and a 3 and 2 count with the Cubs leading, 4-3. Bob Robertson swung at the pitch and missed, which meant that St Louis would get their chance on thursday to tie the Pirates. But as people dwelled on all the possibilities the most astonishing thing happened. The ball got away from catcher Steve Swisher and Robertson ran to first as Sanguillen scored the tying run. A desperate throw by Swisher to the first baseman hit Robertson in the shoulder and he was safe at first. This game would go to extra innings.

In the bottom of the tenth, Al Oliver, the second batter, belted a pitch into the leftfield corner for a triple. Nothing would stop him from making it to third. The Cubs decided to

Al Oliver   **#16**

play percentage baseball and walked Stargell and Clines to load the bases to set up a force play at any base. Manny Sanguillen then toppled a roller to third baseman Bill Madlock and Al Oliver raced home with the NL Eastern Division winning run. Fans jumped all over the field and Three Rivers lived up to its nickname of "The House that Pandemonium Built."

KDKA-radio broadcasted the postgame celebration from the clubhouse. People blew the victory horn and team officials drowned in champagne. Al Oliver summed it up, "The writers gave up on us and the fans gave up on us. But we didn't give up on ourselves."

That last game typified the Pirates ability to fight their way back into contention. They roared right back after almost falling out of the race. That made Pirate baseball something special.

As KDKA put it, "Pirate baseball is a Series business!"

Bruce Kison   **#25**

Game three 1974 NLCS

```
   PITTSBURGH           LOS ANGELES
        ab r h bi              ab r h bi
Stennett 2b  5 1 1 0   Lopes 2b    3 0 0 0
Sanguillen c 5 0 1 0   Buckner lf  3 0 0 0
A Oliver cf  3 1 1 0   Mota lf     1 0 0 0
Stargell lf  5 2 2 3   Wynn cf     3 0 0 0
Zisk rf      5 1 2 0   Garvey 1b   4 0 0 0
Clines rf    0 0 0 0   W Crwfrd rf 2 0 0 0
B Robrtsn 1b 5 1 0 0   Paciorek rf 1 0 1 0
Hebner 3b    3 1 2 3   Cey 3b      4 0 0 0
Mendoza ss   3 0 1 1   Ferguson c  3 0 0 0
Kison p      3 0 0 0   Russell ss  4 0 2 0
R Hnandz p   1 0 0 0   Rau p       0 0 0 0
                       Hough p     0 0 0 0
                       Joshua ph   0 0 0 0
                       Downing p   1 0 0 0
                       McMullen ph 1 0 0 0
                       Solomon p   0 0 0 0
                       Auerbach ph 1 0 1 0

  Total  38 7 10 7     Total  31 0 4 0
Hebner awarded first on catcher's inter-
ference.
Pittsburgh        502 000 000 — 7
Los Angeles       000 000 000 — 0
  E - Garvey, Hough, Lopes, Ferguson,
Downing, Mendoza. DP - Los Angeles 3.
LOB - Pittsburgh 8, Los Angeles 10. 2B -
Sanguillen, Auerbach. HR - Stargell (1),
Hebner (1).
                IP   H R ER BB SO
Kison (W,1-0)   6 2-3 2 0  0  6  5
R. Hernandz     2 1-3 2 0  0  0  1
Rau (L,0-1)     2-3  3 5  3  1  0
Hough           2 1-3 4 2  2  0  2
Downing         4    1 0  0  1  0
Solomon         2    2 0  0  1  1
  PB - Sanguillen.  T—2:41.  A - 55,953.
```

BRING ON THE DODGERS!

After that scintillating finish in the bottom of the ninth of game 162 to clinch the division pennant, Pirate fans yearned for another chance in the NLCS, this time against the Los Angeles Dodgers. Everyone wanted to get back into the World Series after losing on that wild pitch in 1972.

Pittsburgh's Pirates had a lot to celebrate about their regular season. Statistically speaking, they did very well compared to the 1973 campaign.

Firstly, the outfield amazed everyone as all three starters batted over .300. How many times have you seen that on a baseball squad? Al Oliver lead the way with a .321 average, good enough for second place in the NL batting race, as well as 11 homers and 85 rbi; Richie Zisk sported a .313 average with 17 homers and 100 rbi; and Willie Stargell had a .301 mark with 25 homers and 96 rbi. So that was some offensive outfield!

Yet the other hitters also did very well. Rennie Stennett and Richie Hebner both had .291 batting averages. Hebner also added 18 homers and 68 rbi. Manny Sanguillen added another 68 rbi with a .287 average. Dominican Frank Taveras performed very well for a rookie, compiling a .246 batting average. Bob Robertson added 16 homers and 48 rbi with a .229 mark. Naturally, Dave Parker also contributed with a .282 mark as he learned the National League.

The pitching also improved greatly from the previous year. All the starters finished at .500 or better for the regular season. How many teams can ever say that? Jerry Reuss lead the way with a 16-11 mark and a 3.50 era; Jim Rooker had a 15-11 mark and a 2.78 era; Ken Brett had a 13-9 mark and a 2.20 era; Dock Ellis checked in at 12-9 and a 3.16 mark; Bruce Kison had a 9-8 record with a 3.49 era; and the rookie Larry Demery finished at 6-6 with a 4.25 era. The relief pitching still stood solid with Dave Giusti, Ramon Hernandez and Bruce Kison.

So the Pirates, despite their struggle to win the division, had many positive factors that gave them confidence going against the Dodgers in the 1974 NLCS.

Naturally, the Dodgers had quite a team, lead by 1974 All-Star MVP and regular season NL MVP Steve Garvey at first base, Davey Lopes at second, Bill Russell at short and Ron Cey at third. Many consider that one of the best infields ever.

Yet the outfield also had some good bats with Jim "Toy Canon" Wynn and Bill Buckner.

But the pitching also stood as the Dodgers highlight. With starters Don Sutton and Andy Messermith and Mike Marshall in the bullpen, Los Angeles could shut down any team in a short series.

So the Pirates had a formidable foe for the NLCS.

MLB set the starting time for the first game at 1:00 on October 5th at Three Rivers Stadium. Curt Gowdy and Tony Kubek would be there for that first contest to give all the details to the general public. The Pirates felt good about their chances because they had defeated the Dodgers in all six of the regular season meetings between the teams during the regular season.

Amazingly, the weather was so cold that it snowed this early in Pittsburgh for the first time since 1895. Everyone wondered what would happen if Pittsburgh hosted the World Series again.

Don Sutton hurled against Jerry Reuss in the opener in a matchup of the team's two aces.

Don whitewashed the Pirates by a 3-0 score, allowing only four hits. Pirate bats threatened only once as Jimmy Wynn made a spectacular catch on a drive off of the bat of Jerry Reuss.

Yet the Dodgers didn't exactly light it up offensively either. Jerry Reuss gave up only one run on a walk in eight innings of work. Dave Giusti then gave up two more runs in the top of the ninth and that decided the issue.

Taking this game meant much to the Dodgers because it guaranteed them a split of the first two games in Pittsburgh.

But the Dodgers did better than getting a split.

In the second game, on Sunday, October 6th, the Pirates and Dodgers had a 2-2 tie in the seventh on a groundout by Hebner and single by Oliver that broke the 15-inning scoreless streak by the Pirates against Andy Messersmith. In the top of the eighth, the Pirates played sloppily and gave up three runs behind the relief pitching of Dave Giusti. Many observers considered it the sloppiest baseball since early May. A headline in one Pittsburgh paper read,"Gloom on a Sunny Day at Three Rivers." Mike Marshall, who appeared in a record 106 games during the regular season, shut down the Pirate bats. Dodger Ron Cey had a homer, two doubles and a single.

Bruce Kison then shut down the Dodger bats with 6 2/3 frames of shutout ball in the third game at Dodger Stadium. Dodger Doug Rau lasted 2/3 of an inning and only ten minutes as lefty swingers Richie Hebner and Willie Stargell both homered in the 7-0 victory. It was Willie's first homer in postseason play and Hebner's roundtripper was a two-run shot.

Before that game, Bruce Kison declared,"It's a big game, the biggest of the year. The percentages are not in our favor, but it's been that way a lot of times this year. All I can do is give them the best I've got for as long as I can." He definitely did just that in this 7-0 shutout as he stretched his streak to 19 2/3 innings without giving up a run in postseason play.

Next came the crucial Game Four. The Pirates had to win again to send the NLCS to Game Five. So there was pressure.

It turned into Sutton death for the Pirates as Don hurled a four-hitter in the Dodgers 12-1 victory. That triumph set a record for the largest winning margin in NLCS play and gave Sutton a 2-0 record with an 0.53 era in 17 innings. Basically, he shut down the Buccos completely. The three .300 hitting Pirate outfielders certainly didn't do much against him! Steve Garvey had two homers and two singles to go with 4 rbi for the game.

So the Dodgers went on to face the A's in an all-California World Series and the Pirates had to reload for next year.

But they had a lot of highlights that gave them optimism to come back stronger in 1975.

Why did the Pirates lose to the Dodgers in four games?

Perhaps one reason focused on the Pirates having three lefthanded starters against their righthanded power of Garvey, Cey, Wynn, Ferguson and company. After all, Jim Wynn and Steve Garvey both eclipsed 100 rbi for the season with 111 and 108, respectively. That might have had something to do with it, although it certainly wasn't the whole story.

Certainly the loss of Dock Ellis to injury hampered the pitching staff. Before he got hurt, he had won nine out of ten decisions. He also owned an 11-2 lifetime record against LA. Things could have changed if Ellis had mowed down the Dodgers as Sutton shut down the Pirates.

The season may have ended prematurely, but the Buccos sure had a lot of positives.

Rennie Stennett sure emerged as a true talent with a .291 average and 196 hits, a club record for second basemen. GM Joe L. Brown had this to say,"There hasn't been a player in baseball, not even Pete Rose, who has hustled more than Stennett has this year." His quickness, agility and speed made him one of the league's best second sackers. In fact, he had a string of 59 games without an error and lead the league in putouts with 441.

The platooning of Ed Kirkpatrick and Bob Robertson at first base made sense because they complemented each other beautifully. Kirkpatrick got several clutch hits, while hitting a respectable .247 with 6 homers and 38 rbi. He also displayed the type of hustle you're looking for. Bob Robertson got back into the groove somewhat with 16 homers and 48 rbi.

Ed Kirkpatrick   **#23**

More than that, Frank Taveras solved the Pirates' shortstop dilemma. They acquired Dal Maxvill, Paul Popovich, Mario Mendoza and others to fill the void left by the departure of Alley and Hernandez. Taveras batted .246 in his rookie season and learned the position well. His basestealing skills began to emerge as he finished second on the club to Clines with fourteen.

Other guys also contributed. Paul Popovich contributed with clutch pinchhitting. Mario Mendoza and Art Howe also performed well. Ken Macha, a Monroeville product, also helped with a .600 batting average as he went three for five.

Al Oliver finished second in the NL batting race with a .321 average and collected 198 hits, good for fourth in the loop. On top of that, he finished fifth in the NL in total bases with 293. Amazingly, through September 25th, he had hit safely in 114 of 140 games. He did not go more than two consecutive games without a hit. The team gave him the name of "Batman," as he hit safely in 21 straight games.

The other member of that dynamic duo answered to the name of Richie Zisk with the nickname of "RBI man." He compiled a 20-game hitting streak at the same time as Al had at 21 game mark. Richie collected 100 rbi on 168 hits and with only 17 homers. That showed his clutch hitting ability with runners on base. Amazingly, he lead the Pirates in rbi and finished fifth in the batting race.

Dave Parker spent most of the season off the field due to injury. But he showed that he had all the tools you could hope for. As one observer related,"He is exceptionally fast for a big man, a great power hitter and is built like a brick wall." Most Pirate fans hoped to see him in the lineup more often. He started the season at first base and compiled stats of 4 homers, 29 rbi and a .282 batting average.

Stargell hit .301 and had 25 homers with 96 rbi, a good season but not a great one. He floundered in mediocrity for a while. But in the playoffs he exploded with two homers and hit safely in each of the four games.

Hebner had a decent year with 18 homers, 68 rbi and a .291 average but his defense suffered as he lead the league's third basemen in errors with 28. Many of those errors hurt deeply, including one in the NLCS.

Manny Sanguillen had a sub-par year with a .287 average with 6 homers and 68 rbi. But he regained his throwing arm and threw out basestealers left and right. Lou Brock, who set the NL record for steals with 118 in 1974, even acknowledged that Sanguillen was the most difficult catcher to steal against.

After reflecting on the season, GM Joe L. Brown decided to make some more deals.

Shortly after losing to the Dodgers in the NLCS, Brown traded Gene Clines to the Mets for catcher Duffy Dyer. This would satisfy both teams since the Pirates had an abundance of power-hitting outfielders now and Gene would no longer get much playing time. After the trade, Clines admitted,"With the Pirates, it was power, power, power. I was the only guy who could steal a base. Everybody knew it too, and that made it tougher on me. But speed is my biggest asset and running is my game, so the Mets will be my kind of team."

Clines added, "It was always June or July before I got my chance. I'd sit there for two months and do nothing, then they expected me to come in and hit .300. You can't do that all the time. You get rusty."

On top of that, Gene interjected,"The Mets need outfielders and I plan to be a starter for them. I'd prefer centerfield but if it is left or right it is all right by me. I think they will take advantage of my speed and that is something that never happened here."

The Pirates would get a good backup in Dyer, as Joe L. Brown observed, "We think that Duffy Dyer will be a good solid backup for Manny Sanguillen. Not only has he proven himself an excellent receiver and a good handler of pitchers, but I feel he's a better hitter than his average indicates."

Despite Dyer's .211 lifetime batting average, Brown added, "A rested Sanguillen will help us too. I think here he will prove to be a better hitter. He will be surrounded by hitters and that should help his average."

On December 4th, the Pirates picked up pitcher Jim Ray from Detroit for cash. The hope was to get Giusti more help in the bullpen yet he never actually hurled for the Pirates.

Three Pirates pitchers had to have offseason surgery to repair problems, Dave Giusti, John Morlan and Ken Brett. Bob Robertson would also go under the knife. Team doctor Albert Ferguson performed the surgery.

Dave Giusti's elbow problems resulted from a bone chip in his right elbow that made it uncomfortable to pitch. His surgery did not seem serious but was necessary. He admitted that the elbow bothered him during the last two weeks of the season and into the playoffs. Giusti was sidelined from September 9th until the 19th. Dave recalled,"The elbow didn't respond when I pitched after the layoff in September."

John Morlan's surgery stood as serious because Dr. Ferguson would have to cut tissue to remove bone chips in his right elbow.

Brett's elbow problems kept him out of the rotation for over a month so it was critical for him. When he returned from the injured list, he won his first contest and then lost the rest.

Bob Robertson went through a knee operation in the offseason to see if he could regain his form of '70 and '71.

The Buccos revealed that Bob Moose would work out in the Instructional League to get back into shape after surgery for a blood clot. He would add a lot to the staff if he could come back.

Somehow, everyone also hoped that Steve Blass would rebound from his 2-9 record and 9.74 era with Charleston to get back to the big leagues. Reportedly, he went to see Dr. Bill Harrison of Davis, California, to learn the optometherapy, which is concentrating on the task at hand. He spent four days with him because he couldn't face a batter. Steve also tried TM and other things.

One absurdity, which Myron Cope reported on one Sunday evening newscast for channel 4, had the Pirates ready to trade Stargell to the Phillies for Willie Montanez and Jim Lonborg, a previous Cy Young Award winner. People really wondered. Would the Pirates trade their most awesome power hitter away?

Bob Prince went to the hospital and came out fine. He would be ready for "Babushka Power" and the "Drive for Five."

Pirate management hoped to see the attendance increase the next year. The Pirates made the playoffs and drew only 1.1 million fans. The Reds, who finished second to the Dodgers, had 2 million fans. Many of the Pirates admitted that the low attendance bothered them.

TEAM BATTING

TEAM	AVG	HR	2B	3B	SA	SB
Pittsburgh Pirates	.274	114	238	46	.391	55
Los Angeles Dodgers	.272	139	231	34	.401	149
St Louis Cardinals	.265	83	216	46	.365	172
Houston Astros	.263	110	222	41	.378	108
Philadelphia Phillies	.261	95	233	50	.373	115
Cincinnati Reds	.260	135	271	35	.394	146
Montreal Expos	.254	86	201	29	.350	124
San Francisco Giants	.252	93	228	38	.358	107
Chicago Cubs	.251	110	221	42	.365	78
Atlanta Braves	.249	120	202	37	.363	72
New York Mets	.235	96	183	22	.329	43
San Diego Padres	.229	99	196	27	.330	85

TEAM PITCHING

TEAM	ERA	CG	BB	SO	ShO	SV
Los Angeles Dodgers	2.97	33	464	943	19	23
Atlanta Braves	3.05	46	488	772	21	22
Cincinnati Reds	3.42	34	536	875	11	27
New York Mets	3.42	46	504	908	15	14
Houston Astros	3.48	36	601	738	18	18
St Louis Cardinals	3.48	37	616	794	13	20
Pittsburgh Pirates	3.49	51	543	721	9	17
Montreal Expos	3.60	35	544	822	8	27
San Francisco Giants	3.80	27	559	756	11	25
Chicago Cubs	4.28	23	576	895	6	26
San Diego Padres	4.61	25	715	855	7	19

TEAM FIELDING

TEAM	FA	E	DP
Houston Astros	.982	113	161
Atlanta Braves	.979	132	161
Cincinnati Reds	.979	134	51
St Louis Cardinals	.977	147	192
Philadelphia Phillies	.976	148	168
Montreal Expos	.976	153	157
New York Mets	.975	158	50
Pittsburgh Pirates	.975	162	154
Los Angeles Dodgers	.975	157	122
San Diego Padres	.973	170	126
San Francisco Giants	.972	175	153
Chicago Cubs	.969	199	41

NL INDIVIDUAL HITTING

PLAYER	AVG	AB	H	2B	3B	HR	R	RBI	BB	SO	SB
Garr, Ralph	.353	606	214	24	17	11	87	54	28	52	26
Oliver, Al	.321	617	198	38	12	11	96	85	33	58	0
Gross, Greg	.314	589	185	21	8	0	78	36	76	39	12

Buckner, Bill	.314	580	182	30	3	7	83	58	30	24	31
Zisk, Richie	.313	536	168	30	3	17	75	100	65	91	1
Garvey, Steve	.312	642	200	2	3	21	95	111	31	66	5
McBride, Bake	.309	559	173	19	5	6	8	56	43	57	30
Smith, Reggie	.309	517	160	26	9	23	9	100	71	70	4
Brock, Lou	.306	635	194	25	7	3	105	48	61	88	118
Montanez, Willie	.304	527	160	33	1	7	55	79	32	57	3
Stargell, Willie	.301	508	153	37	4	25	90	96	87	106	0
Cash, Dave	.300	687	206	26	11	2	89	58	46	33	20
Watson, Bob	.298	524	156	19	4	11	69	67	69	61	3
Crawford, Willie	.295	468	128	23	4	11	73	61	64	88	7
Davis, Willie	.295	611	180	27	9	12	86	89	27	69	25
Monday, Rick	.294	538	158	19	7	20	84	58	70	94	
Cardenal, Jose	.293	542	159	35	3	13	75	72	56	67	23
Morgan, Joe	.293	512	150	31	3	22	107	67	120	69	58
Stennett, Rennie	.291	673	196	29	3	7	84	56	32	51	8
Hebner, Richie	.291	550	160	21	6	18	97	68	60	53	0
Matthews, Gary	.287	561	161	27	6	16	87	82	70	69	11
Sanguillen, Manny	.287	596	171	21	4	7	77	68	21	27	2
Maddox, Gary	.284	538	153	31	3	8	74	50	29	64	21
Rose, Pete	.284	652	185	45	7	3	110	51	106	54	2
Schmidt, Mike	.282	568	160	28	7	36	108	116	106	138	23

NL INDIVIDUAL PITCHING

PLAYER	ERA	W-L	G	GS	CG	IP	H	BB	SO	ShO	SV
Capra, Buzz	2.28	16-8	39	27	11	217	163	84	137	5	1
Niekro, Phil	2.38	20-13	41	39	18	302	249	88	195	6	1
Matlack, Jon	2.41	13-15	34	34	14	265	221	76	195	7	0
Marshall, Mike	2.42	15-12	106	0	0	208	191	56	143	0	21
Messersmith, Andy	2.59	20-6	39	39	13	292	227	94	221	3	0
McGlothen, Lynn	2.69	16-12	31	31	8	237	212	89	142	3	0
Barr, Jim	2.74	13-9	44	27	11	240	223	47	84	5	2
Rooker, Jim	2.78	15-11	33	33	15	263	228	83	139	1	0
Dierker, Larry	2.90	11-10	33	33	7	224	189	82	150	3	0
Caldwell, Mike	2.95	14-5	31	27	6	189	176	63	83	2	0
Gullett, Don	3.04	17-11	36	35	10	243	201	88	183	3	0
Wilson, Don	3.08	11-13	33	27	5	205	170	100	112	4	0
Norman, Fred	3.14	13-12	35	26	8	186	170	68	141	2	0
Morton, Carl	3.15	16-12	38	38	7	275	293	89	113	1	0
Ellis, Dock	3.16	12-9	26	26	9	177	163	41	91	0	0
Seaver, Tom	3.20	11-11	32	32	12	236	199	75	201	5	0
Lonborg, Jim	3.21	17-13	39	39	16	283	280	70	121	3	0
Carlton, Steve	3.22	16-13	39	39	17	291	249	136	240	1	0
Sutton, Don	3.23	19-9	40	40	10	276	241	80	179	5	0
Kirby, Clay	3.28	12-9	36	35	7	231	210	91	160	1	0
Brett, Ken	3.30	13-9	27	27	10	191	192	53	96	3	0
Koosman, Jerry	3.36	15-11	35	35	13	265	258	85	188	0	0
Reed, Ron	3.39	10-11	28	28	6	186	171	41	78	2	0

Roberts, Dave	3.40	10-12	34	30	8	204	216	65	72	2	1
Reuss, Jerry	3.50	16-11	35	35	14	260	259	10	105	1	0

PIRATE HITTING STATS

Player	AVG	a/b	r	h	2b	3b	HR	RBI	BB	SO	SB
Macha, Ken	.600	5	1	3	1	0	0	1	0	0	0
Oliver, Al	.321	617	96	198	38	12	11	85	33	58	10
Zisk, Richie	.313	536	75	168	30	3	17	100	65	91	1
Brett, Ken	.310	87	*	27	*	*	2	*	*	*	*
Rooker, Jim	.305	95	*	29	*	*	0	*	*	*	*
Stargell, Willie	.301	508	90	153	37	4	25	96	87	106	0
Hebner, Richie	.291	550	97	160	21	6	18	68	60	53	0
Stennett, Rennie	.291	673	84	196	29	3	7	56	32	51	8
Sanguillen, Manny	.287	596	77	171	21	4	7	68	21	27	2
Parker, Dave	.282	220	27	62	10	3	4	29	10	53	3
Hernandez, Ramon	.250	4	*	1	*	*	0	*	*	*	*
Kirkpatrick, Ed	.247	271	32	67	9	0	6	38	51	30	1
Taveras, Frank	.246	333	33	82	4	2	0	26	25	41	13
Howe, Art	.243	74	10	18	4	1	1	5	15	15	1
Clines, Gene	.225	276	29	62	5	1	0	14	30	40	14
Mendoza, Mario	.221	163	10	36	1	2	0	15	13	20	2
Popovich, Paul	.217	83	9	18	2	1	0	5	5	10	0
Ellis, Dock	.214	56	*	12	*	*	*	*	*	*	*
Maxvill, Dal	.182	*	*	*	*	*	0	0	*	*	0
Augustine, Dave	.182	22	3	4	5	0	0	0	0	0	0
Mose, Bob	.182	11	*	*	*	0	*	*	*	*	
Demery, Larry	.152	35	*	5	*	*	0	0	0	0	0
Reuss, Jerry	.151	86	*	13	*	*	0	*	*	*	*
Brinkman, Chuck	.143	21	2	3	0	0	0	1	1	3	0
Bevacqua, Kurt	.114	*	*	*	*	*	0	0	0	0	0
Giusti, Dave	.111	9	*	1	*	*	0	*	*	*	*
Kison, Bruce	.108	37	*	4	*	*	0	*	*	*	*
Ryan, Mike	.100	30	2	3	0	0	0	0	4	16	0
Ott, Ed	.000	5	1	0	0	0	0	0	0	0	0
Dilone, Miguel	.000	2	3	0	0	0	0	0	1	0	2

PIRATE PITCHING STATS

PITCHER	ERA	W-L	G	GS	CG	IP	H	R	ER	BB	SO	SV
Minshall, Jim	0.00	0-1	5	0	0	4	1	1	0	2	3	0
Pizarro, Juan	1.88	1-1	7	2	0	24	20	*	*	11	7	0
Hernandez, Ramon	2.75	5-2	58	0	0	69	68	21	21	18	33	2
Rooker, Jim	2.78	15-11	33	33	15	263	228	93	81	83	139	0
Ellis, Dock	3.16	12-9	26	26	9	177	163	*	*	41	91	0
Brett, Ken	3.30	13-9	27	27	10	191	192	*	*	53	96	0
Giusti, Dave	3.32	7-5	64	2	0	106	101	43	39	40	53	12
Kison, Bruce	3.49	9-8	40	16	1	129	123	64	50	57	71	2
Reuss, Jerry	3.50	16-11	35	35	14	260	259	115	101	101	105	0
Demery, Larry	4.25	6-6	19	15	2	115	95	40	37	43	59	0

Morlan, John	4.29	0-3	39	0	0	65	54	*	*	48	38	0
Sadowski, Jim	6.00	0-1	4	0	0	9	7	*	*	9	1	0
Tekulve, Kent	6.00	1-1	8	0	0	9	12	6	6	5	6	0
Jiminez, Juan	6.75	0-0	4	0	0	4	6	*	*	2	2	0
Patterson, Daryl	7.29	2-1	14	0	0	21	35	*	*	9	8	1
Moose, Bob	7.57	1-5	7	6	0	36	59	30	30	7	15	0
Blass, Steve	9.00	0-0	1	0	0	5	5	*	*	7	2	0

1975 Schedule

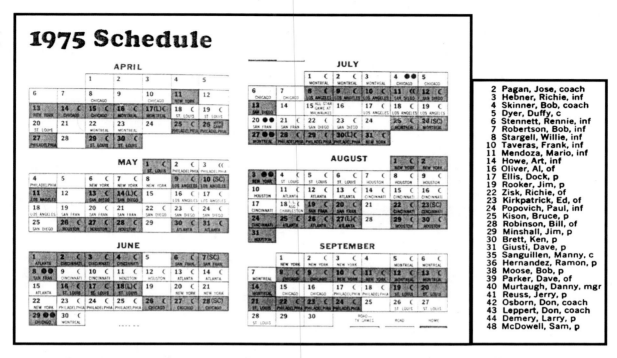

2	Pagan, Jose, coach
3	Hebner, Richie, inf
4	Skinner, Bob, coach
5	Dyer, Duffy, c
6	Stennett, Rennie, inf
7	Robertson, Bob, inf
8	Stargell, Willie, inf
10	Taveras, Frank, inf
11	Mendoza, Mario, inf
14	Howe, Art, inf
16	Oliver, Al, of
17	Ellis, Dock, p
19	Rooker, Jim, p
22	Zisk, Richie, of
23	Kirkpatrick, Ed, of
24	Popovich, Paul, inf
25	Kison, Bruce, p
28	Robinson, Bill, of
29	Minshall, Jim, p
30	Brett, Ken, p
31	Giusti, Dave, p
35	Sanguillen, Manny, c
36	Hernandez, Ramon, p
38	Moose, Bob, p
39	Parker, Dave, of
40	Murtaugh, Danny, mgr
41	Reuss, Jerry, p
42	Osborn, Don, coach
43	Leppert, Don, coach
44	Demery, Larry, p
48	McDowell, Sam, p

THE DRIVE FOR FIVE IN '75

Optimism reigned in 1975 as the Pirate Ship readied for another assault on the National League. After getting back to the top of the division in 1974, the Pirates made some subtle changes in their roster to make another run.

Before spring training began, Joe L. Brown performed some more magic by acquiring Sudden Sam McDowell, a Pittsburgh native. McDowell would join the Pirates in training camp on February 21st as a non-roster player, which meant that it would cost the Buccos nothing. That excited Pirate fans to know that the tenth leading strikeout pitcher of all-time with 2,424 k's would

Sam McDowell   **#48**

join their team. His 8.88 strikeout per game mark stood second only to Sandy Koufax on the all-time list at the time. That certainly got the Pirate fans talking.

During spring training, the Pirates sported an 18-17 mark, good for a .514 winning percentage.

But the heartbreaking event of the spring came on March 24, 1975, when Steve Blass hurled for the last time. He started the second game of a doubleheader against the Chicago White Sox and looked okay in the early going. Steve gave up two runs in the second frame and even struck out slugger Bill Melton. But then Blass fell apart in the fourth when he walked eight batters and gave up eight runs. He threw one pitch behind Carlos May on a 3-2 pitch. He only threw 17 strikes out of 51 pitches and the booing got bad. Steve Blass could not get the third out and Giusti relieved him.

Three days later the Pirates put him on waivers and no one claimed him. Blass finally retired after working with minor league pitching coach Larry Sherry, Dr. Bill Harrison again and Arthur Ellen, a hypnotist. Nothing seemed to help.

No baseball player ever fell so far so fast after being at the top of his game.

Then just before the regular season began, Brown made another trade, sending pitcher Wayne Simpson to the Phillies for outfielder Bill Robinson, who would become a big contributor to the Pirates over the years. Little did Pirate fans know how important this trade would be down the road.

The Pirates opened their 1975 season on the road at Wrigley Field and won 8-4 as Dave Giusti picked up the win. Stargell launched two homers and the Pirates hit four as a team. Things looked good for the Buccos.

The Buccos then came home and won two straight from the Mets by scores of 4-3 and 5-3. Larry Demery defeated Rick Baldwin and Bruce Kison outlasted Tom Seaver.

So this modest three-game winning streak got the Pirate Ship sailing in the right direction.

Next came a four-game losing streak.

The Pirates lost to the Cubs by a 4-2 count on the 14th of April, then Woodie Fryman of the Expos shut them out by a 5-0 score on the 16th, both at Three Rivers. Dave McNally then defeated the Pirates 7-4 on the 17th defeating another lefthander- Jerry Reuss. On the 18th, Ray Sadecki outhurled Sam McDowell, 5-4. So the Pirates went from first to fourth place in four games.

Jim Rooker got the Buccos out of their losing ways with a 7-1 triumph over Bob Forsch on the 18th at Busch Stadium.

Then Ken Brett whitewashed the Cardinals and John Denny by a 5-0 count.

So things looked good for the Buccos.

At Parc Jarry, the Expos took two from the Pirates by scores of 4-3 and 5-0. Dave McNally defeated Dock Ellis and Woodie Fryman triumphed over Jerry Reuss.

The good thing was that the Pirates would finish out April at home at Three Rivers Stadium against the Phillies and Cardinals.

Bruce Kison showed his poise in defeating Steve Carlton by a 3-2 count on April 25th. Dave Giusti picked up the save. The following night, Jim Rooker triumphed over Wayne Twitchell by a margin of 7-3. Dock Ellis then got the broom out the next night to complete the sweep with a 2-0 shutout against tom Underwood.

The Cardinals then came to town. Lynn McGlothen whitewashed the Buccos by a 3-0 count on April 29th. Then Jerry Reuss returned the favor as he shutout Bob Gibson by a 5-0 score.

So the Pirates finished April with a 9-7 record , which was good enough for second place.

May commenced with a roadtrip to divisional foes Philadelphia and New York.

Surprisingly, the Phillies swept us at Veteran's Stadium by a score of 9-5, and then in a doubleheader by 6-2 and 4-3. Wayne Twitchell got the first win, Tom Underwood the second and Tug McGraw the third while Bruce Kison, Jim Rooker and Ramon Hernandez got credited with the losses.

The Buccos then swept the Mets at Shea Stadium, commencing with a great 2-1 win by Ken Brett over Tom Seaver on the 6th of May. Jerry Reuss then outhurled Jon Matlack by a 6-1 count the following day. Bruce Kison bested Jerry Koosman by a 4-2 score on May 8th.

Then it was time to return home to the confluence.

Dock Ellis evened his record at 2-2 with an easy 11-3 triumph over the Dodgers and Mike Marshall. Dave Giusti picked up the save as the Pirates won their fourth in a row and improved their record to 13-10.

The next two games did not go well however. Doug Rau won 6-2 over the Pirates and Jim Rooker on the 10th. Then Don Sutton picked up where he left off in the playoffs with a 7-0 shutout the next game as Ken Brett got the loss.

San Diego came to town for a two-game set and the Pirates started two lefties against them. Jerry Reuss shut out the Padres, 2-0, in the May 13th contest. Then Sudden Sam McDowell got his first win in a Pirate uniform with a 5-4 triumph on the 14th.

Then, on the first part of a west coast roadtrip, the Pirates took two out of three from the Dodgers. We finally defeated Don Sutton by a 3-2 count on the 16th of May as Dave Giusti got the win. After losing to Andy Messersmith by a 4-3 margin on the 17th, Ken Brett defeated Burt Hooton on the 18th by a 7-2 score.

On the second stop of the west coast swing, the Giants swept the Pirates at Candlestick Park. Mike Caldwell defeated Jerry Reuss on the 19th by a 6-4 margin. Then the Giants lambasted the Buccos by a 12-4 count on the 20th as only 1,759 showed up for the game at Candlestick, the smallest road crowd of the season. Jim Barr won a

2-1 squeaker in the third contest.

Next came a four-game series at San Diego's Jack Murphy Stadium. The Pirates and Padres split a four-game series. The Pirates won the first game 4-2 behind the pitching of Jim Rooker and the relief of Dave Giusti. Then the Padres won the middle two games by scores of 4-3 and 5-0, as Randy Jones hurled shutout ball in the latter game. Then Ramon Hernandez got the win and Larry Demery the save in the 6-5 triumph in the last game of the series.

That last win ignited a six-game winning streak, the longest of the season.

In the Astros series at Three Rivers, the Pirates won the three games in convincing fashion. Bruce Kison defeated 6 foot 8 inch flame-thrower J.R. Richard by a 10-2 count in the first contest. Larry Demery triumphed over Joe Niekro by a 6-5 margin in the second. Then Ken Brett shutout Dave Roberts, 3-0.

Next came the Atlanta Braves.

Jerry Reuss evened his record at 4-4 in defeating Buzz Capra, 2-1. Then Bruce Kison outhurled Roric Harrison on May 31st, 11-4.

For the month of May, the Pirates had a 15-11 record and an overall mark of 24-18. They resided in first place as well.

June 1st started with a 5-2 loss to the Braves in the final game of that series as knuckleballer Phil Niekro defeated Jim Rooker.

The Reds came to town for a series and won the first game 8-4 behind Gary Nolan, as Bob Moose lost his second game. Jerry Reuss won the next game, 2-1, as Ramon Hernandez got the save and Fred Norman absorbed the loss.

San Francisco came to town for a four-game series and the two teams split. The Buccos won the first two games of the series by margins of 7-2 and 7-6 as Bruce Kison and Ramon Hernandez got the victories on June 6th and 7th. On Sunday, June 8th, the Pirates actually lost a doubleheader to the Giants by 3-1 and 4-2 scores as Ed Halicki and Gary Lavelle both won. John Candelaria lost the first game of his career in that first game of the doubleheader. The Pirates regained first place and would stay there the remainder of the season.

The Bucs traveled to their sister stadium, Riverfront, for a two-game series with the Reds. They took both games, by scores of 9-2 and 9-5, as lefties Jerry Reuss and Sam McDowell got the victories.

In the Astrodome, the Pirates then split a series with the Astros, losing a 5-1 decision to Larry Dierker on the 11th and then defeating the Astros by a 4-2 count as Dock Ellis got credit for the victory.

A trip to Atlanta helped get a nice winning streak going as the Pirates swept a three-game series from the Braves in Atlanta-Fulton County Stadium. On Friday the 13th, not normally a day for good luck, Jim Rooker outhurled former Oakland pitcher John Blue Moon Odom by an 8-3 count. Jerry Reuss outhurled Mike Thompson the next day by a 2-1 margin. Larry Demery then won his third game of the season in an 8-6 victory and got the Bucco winning streak up to four.

Bruce Kison improved the Pirates' record to 34-23 and got the winning streak up to five with a 10-4 triumph the June 16th as he defeated the Cardinals and Ron Bryant at Three Rivers Stadium.

The Buccos took two of the next three from the Cardinals. On June 17th, Lynn McGlothen defeated Dock Ellis by a 7-4 count. But then the lefthanded duo of Jim Rooker and Jerry Reuss triumphed over the Cardinals by scores of 9-3 and 5-0. Jerry Reuss hurled so efficiently in his 5-0 shutout that he actually hurled the shortest game of the year, a 1:40 special.

The Pirate Ship cruised into Shea Stadium for the weekend of June 20-22 and the Pirates got the brooms out for the three-game series, as they swept New York's Mets by scores of 5-1, 7-3 and 2-0. John Candelaria, Ramon Hernandez and Dock Ellis got the victories. That gave the Pirates another five-game winning streak and raised their record to 39-24.

Veteran's Stadium provided the venue for a four-game series against the Phillies from June 23-25 and the crossstate rivals swept a four-game series from the Buccos. In the first game, Tom Hilgendorf defeated Larry Demery by a 6-5 count as former Pirate Gene Garber got the save. Then the Phillies swept the Pirates in a doubleheader on the 24th by scores of 6-3 and 8-1, as Larry Christenson and Tom Underwood triumphed over Jerry Reuss and Bruce Kison. Then Ron Schueler defeated the Pirates and Dave Giusti by a 7-6 margin to bring the Bucco losing streak to four.

John Candelaria stopped that losing streak very quickly the next day at Three Rivers Stadium as he struck out 13 Cub batters, the team high for the season, in a 5-2 triumph. In a strange twist, the Pirates and Cubs would play a six-game series due to rainouts.

A doubleheader sweep, a Pirate trademark during these years, then followed on the 27th as the Buccos defeated the Cubs by scores of 5-1 and 5-3. Dock Ellis and Ramon Hernandez got credit for the victories as the Pirates raised their record to 42-28.

Bill Bonham defeated Jim Rooker by a 1-0 count on Saturday the 28th.

Then the Pirates swept another doubleheader against the Cubs on June 29th, this one by scores of 4-3 and 7-0 as Dave Giusti and Jerry Reuss got the victories. Reuss defeated former Pirate Tom Dettore in his shutout and Dave Giusti triumphed over future Pirate Rick Reuschel.

Larry Demery closed out the month with a 5-3 victory against the Expos in Parc Jarry as Kent Tekulve got his first save of the year.

For the month of June, the Pirates posted a 22-11 mark that raised their overall record to 45-29. The Pirate Ship was on cruise control at this point.

John Candelaria opened the month of July with a 10-4 victory against former Pirate Woodie Fryman.

Then Dock Ellis defeated the Expos by a 5-1 count to get the Pirate winning streak to five as he outhurled Steve Rogers.

Now it was time for the Pirate Ship to cruise into Wrigley for a five-game set.

In a rare occurrence on independence day at Wrigley Field, the Pirates actually lost a doubleheader to the Cubs by scores of 6-1 and 2-1. Steve Stone and Darold Knowles defeated Bruce Kison and Jerry Reuss.

Jim Rooker defeated Ray Burris by a 5-4 count the following day.

Then came the slugfest of the season on July 6th as the Buccos outslugged the Cubs in Wrigley by an 18-12 margin. Amazingly, it stood as the highest run total for the Pirates in a game for the year. Ramon Hernandez got the victory.

Ken Brett whitewashed Rick Reuschel and the Cubs the next day by a 5-0 count as the Pirates got their 50th victory of the season.

Now it was time for the Pirates to return home for a seven-game series.

Los Angeles' Dodgers came to town and Don Sutton continued his mastery over the Pirates with a 3-0 shutout against Dock Ellis. But Bruce Kison outhurled Andy Messersmith the next day in a 3-2 victory. Jerry Reuss got his tenth victory of the season in a 4-1 triumph over Burt Hooton on July 10th.

San Diego's Padres then came to town for a four-game series. Jim Rooker and John Candelaria hurled the Pirates to another doubleheader sweep on the 11th by scores of 6-2 and 5-0. On the 12th, Ramon Hernandez got credit for the 6-4 victory to get the Pirates another five-game winning streak and improve their record to 55-32. Then the Buccos lost the last game of the series by a 7-5 margin as Brent Strom defeated Dock Ellis.

Now it was time for the All-Star break and the Pirates stood in first place.

For the second time in five years, a Pirate would start the All-Star Game. Jerry Reuss started the July 15th game in Milwaukee against AL lefthander Vida Blue.

Other Pirate representatives included Al Oliver, who made it for the second time as a Pirate, and Manny Sanguillen, who made it for his third time.

The National League won 6-3 by getting three runs in the top of the ninth. Jerry Reuss pitched three innings without giving up a run and the two teams stood tied at 3-3 in the eighth. In the ninth, Reggie Smith lead off with a single that Claudell Washington dropped. Al Oliver then pinchit for Jon Matlack and doubled to left to score Smith. Goose Gossage then came in to face Larry Bowa and hit him with a pitch. Bill Madlock then singled to left to bring home two runs. Pete Rose brought home the third tally with a sacrifice fly. Randy Jones came in to shut down the AL in the bottom of the ninth. Future Pirate Bill Madlock and Met Jon Matlack tied for the MVP Award. Steve Garvey and Jim Wynn hit homers for the NL while Carl Yastrzemski hit a roundtripper for the AL.

After the All-Star break, it was time for an eight game west coast roadtrip, always a difficult thing for the eastern division teams.

But the Pirates showed they were ready with a 5-2 victory in the opening game at Dodger Stadium. Bruce Kison defeated Andy Messersmith and Dave Giusti got his twelfth save.

Mike Marshall defeated the Pirates and Larry Demery by a 4-3 count the next day.

Dave Giusti, however, picked up the victory in the rubber game of the series in a 5-3 triumph over Mike Marshall.

So the Pirates got through the first part of the roadtrip in good shape.

In the three-game series at Candlestick, the Pirates lost two out of three. The Pirates split a doubleheader on July 20th, losing the opener 2-1 and winning the nightcap, 7-1. Jim Rooker took the loss and Ken Brett got the win. On the 21st, Jim Barr defeated John Candelaria by a 7-2 score as the Pirates finished 1-5 for the year at Candlestick Park.

Now it was time for the concluding two games of the roadtrip at San Diego's Jack Murphy Stadium. In the first game, Randy Jones shutout the Pirates by a 1-0 count. In the second game on the 23rd, Dock Ellis defeated Dave Freisleben by an 8-1 margin.

The Pirates then had a long homestand over the next few days against their eastern division rivals, the Expos, Phillies and Mets.

After opening the homestand with a 6-1 victory behind Jerry Reuss' marvelous pitching effort in his eleventh triumph of the year, for the Pirates 60th victory, the Pirates looked ready to put together another winning streak.

Steve Rogers shut down the Pirate bats again on July 26th with a 5-2 victory against Jim Rooker.

But then the Pirates got right back on track with a doubleheader sweep on Sunday, July 27th, by scores of 4-1 and 5-3. Ken Brett and

Jerry Reuss   **#41** Dave Giusti got the victories that improved the

Bucco record to 62-38.

Now the Phillies came to town and the Pirates lost the first two to them by scores of 5-2 and 5-1, as Larry Christenson and Tom Underwood defeated Bruce Kison and Dock Ellis.

But Jerry Reuss showed just why he's the team's ace as he outperformed Steve Carlton in an 8-1 victory that improved his record to 12-6.

On the last day of July, the Mets' Jerry Koosman defeated Jim Rooker by a 6-2 count.

So the Pirates concluded July with a 63-41 overall record and posted an 18-12 mark for the month.

The Pirates had four more games against the Mets in the homestand and they split them. On August 1st, they lost 4-2 to George Stone. Then All-Star MVP Jon Matlack whitewashed the Pirates by a 6-0 score. But they swept a doubleheader on Sunday the 3rd by scores of 5-4, in an extra-inning game that lasted 4:07, and 4-3, as Larry Demery and John Candelaria got the victories.

Now it was time for another roadtrip to St Louis, Houston, Atlanta and Cincinnati, in what people would call the dog days of August. The Pirates struggled mightily, putting together a five-game losing streak and a six-game streak as well. So it was not a good time for the Buccos.

The roadtrip started off poorly as the Buccos lost two out of three to the Cardinals in Busch Stadium. Jack Curtis defeated Jerry Reuss in the first game by a 5-4 count. Jim Rooker then got the victory for the Pirates over Eric Rasmussen in the second game by a 6-1 mark. John Denny for the Cardinals then won the third game with a 4-2 victory over Ken Brett, as the Mad Hungarian, Al Hrabosky, got the save.

Houston's Astrodome proved to be a house of doom for the Pirates as they dropped four consecutive games to the Astros, by scores of 6-1, 5-3, 5-0 and 5-3. Houston outscored the Pirates 21-6 in the series as Dave Roberts, Jim Crawford, Joe Niekro and J.R. Richard got the victories while Bruce Kison, Kent Tekulve, Jerry Reuss and Jim Rooker absorbed the losses. This five-game losing streak dropped the Pirate record to 66-49.

At least John Candelaria triumphed in the first game of the three-game series at Atlanta, by an 8-1 count. But the Pirates fell right back into their losing ways with 4-3 and 6-1 losses to the Braves, as Carl Morton and Tom House got victories.

This horrible roadtrip concluded with four games at Cincinnati's Riverfront Stadium against the Reds, in a preview of the NLCS, and the Buccos lost four more. Gary Nolan defeated Jerry Reuss by a 6-1 count in the first game. Fred Norman then triumphed by an 8-3 mark in the second contest. Jack Billingham raised his record to 14-5 with a 5-3 victory over John Candelaria in the third contest. Then, in the final game of the roadtrip,

Pat Darcy defeated Kison by a 3-1 margin, as Pete Rose singled against Bruce for his 2,500th career hit.

During the trip, the Pirates went from a 65-43 record to a 67-55 mark, which meant that they finished 2-12 on their tour through St Louis, Houston, Atlanta and Cincinnati.

Getting back to Three Rivers truly helped the Pirates as Jerry Reuss hurled a 4-0 shutout on August 19th. Jim Rooker followed that up with a 3-1 victory the following day over Ed Halicki.

On August 22nd, the Pirates swept the Reds in a double dip by scores of 7-2 and 4-2, as Larry Demery and John Candelaria got the victories.

That modest four-game winning streak for the Pirates catapulted them to a 71-55 record.

Bruce Kison took the loss in a 12-7 loss to the Reds the next day but then Jerry Reuss got his 14th victory of the season in a 5-1 triumph over Gary Nolan.

On August 25th, The Braves came to town and Jim Rooker shut them out by a 4-0 score. The following day, Larry Demery got his seventh victory by a score of 7-3 as the first eight Pirates picked up safeties against the Braves, which tied the major league record set three weeks prior by the Phillies. In the third game of the series, The Braves won 6-2, as knuckleballer Phil Niekro defeated fireballer John Candelaria.

The Pirates concluded August and the homestand with a split of the two-game series against the Astros. Larry Dierker defeated the Pirates and Jerry Reuss by a 7-4 margin on August 30th. But Bruce Kison triumphed over Jose Sosa by a 9-6 count on August 31st.

The Pirates actually finished with a subpar 11-17 August and had an overall mark of 74-58.

Tom Seaver got his twentieth victory of the season on September 1st in a 3-0 shutout at Shea Stadium and set a record in the process, reaching 200 strikeouts for an eighth consecutive campaign.

The next two days, however, the Pirates defeated the Mets by scores of 8-4 and 3-1, as Kent Tekulve defeated Jerry Koosman and Jerry Reuss got his 15th victory against Jon Matlack.

In Parc Jarry, the Pirates won three out of four. In a doubleheader on the 5th, the Pirates split with a 4-3 loss in the opener and a 5-2 win in the nightcap. Kent Tekulve absorbed the loss and Jim Rooker got the win. Then the Pirates blew out the Expos in two consecutive contests by scores of 12-5 and 6-0. Ken Brett got the victory on the 6th against Dale Murray and Jerry Reuss hurled another of his marvelous shutouts on the 7th, which got the Buccos to the 80-win plateau.

The Cubs, Mets and Expos then came to Three Rivers Stadium for a nice homestand.

In the Cubs series, Dock Ellis won the first game by a 4-1 count as the Pirate win streak reached four. The Pirates lost to the Cubs, 6-5, the next day, as Bruce Kison hit Bill Madlock with a pitch that fractured his right thumb and put him out for the rest of the season.

The Mets also came to town for a two-game set and the Pirates split that one too. Jim Rooker defeated Tom Seaver on September 10th by an 8-4 margin. Then Jerry Koosman outhurled Jerry Reuss in a 7-0 shutout the next night.

Montreal came to the confluence next, this time for the traditional three-game series. In the Friday night game, Bob Moose defeated Don Carrithers 6-3. The Expos then won 5-2 on September 13th as Dan Warthen defeated Dock Ellis. In the third game of the series, Ramon Hernandez got the win in relief over Woodie Fryman in a 4-3 triumph.

Next came another roadtrip to Chicago and Philadelphia.

Wrigley Field promised some interesting moments for the Pirates.

The Pirates split a doubleheader with the Cubs on September 15th, losing the opener 6-5 and then winning the nightcap by a 9-1 mark. Jim Rooker improved his record to 13-9 in the nightcap.

PIRATES	ab	r	h	bi	CHICAGO	ab	r	h	bi
Stennett, 2b	7	5	7	2	Kessinger, 3b	3	0	0	0
Randolph, 2b	0	0	0	0	Dunn, 3b	1	0	0	0
Hebner, 3b	7	2	2	3	Tyrone, lf	4	0	0	0
A. Oliver, cf	4	2	1	1	JeMorales, cf	3	0	0	0
Dilone, cf	1	0	0	1	LaDock, rf	2	0	1	0
Stargell, 1b	4	2	3	3	Cardenal, rf	2	0	0	0
Robertson, 1b	3	1	1	0	Harris, cf	1	0	0	0
D. Parker, rf	4	3	2	5	Thornton, 1b	3	0	0	0
Zisk, lf	5	2	2	1	P. Reuschel, p	2	0	0	0
Sanguillen, c	3	2	1	0	Trillo, 2b	2	0	0	0
Brett, p	1	0	0	0	Sperring, 2b	1	0	0	0
Taveras, ss	6	1	3	3	Mitterwald, c	3	0	0	0
Candelaria, p	5	1	1	2	Rosello, ss	3	0	1	0
Ott, ph	1	0	0	0	R. Reuschel, p	0	0	0	0
					Dettore, p	1	0	0	0
					Zamora, p	0	0	0	0
					Hosley, ph	1	0	0	0
					Schultz, p	0	0	0	0
					Summers, rf	1	0	0	0
Totals	53	22	24	21	Totals	30	0	3	0

```
PIRATES .......................... 902  162  200—22
CHICAGO .......................... 000  000  000— 0
```

E—Dettore, Rosello, Dunn. LOB—Pirates 12, Chicago 3.
2B—Stennett 2. 3B—Stennett. HR—Hebner (15), D. Parker (24). SF—D. Parker.

	IP	H	R	ER	BB	SO
Candelaria (W, 8-5)	7	3	0	0	0	5
Brett	2	0	0	0	0	1
R. Reuschel (L, 10-16)	1/3	6	8	6	2	0
Dettore	3 1/3	7	8	7	2	0
Zamora	1	4	2	2	0	1
Schultz	2	6	4	2	1	2
P. Reuschel	2	2	1	1	2	0

HBP—by Dettore (D. Parker). WP—Dettore.
T—2:35. A—4,932.

Rennie Stennett   **#6**

Then came the date that will live in infamy in baseball history- September 16, 1975. In the Pirates' 22-0 whitewashing of the Cubs, Rennie Stennett became the only batter in major league history to go seven-for-seven in a nine-inning game. He tied Wilbert Robinson's major league record, which was set on June 10, 1892. Stennett collected two hits in the first and fifth innings and scored five of the Pirate runs in the massacre.

Details of his performance amazed everyone. In the first inning, he doubled to right and singled to right. He followed that up with a single to center in the third. Then, in the fifth frame, he doubled to center and singled to right. Rennie singled to rightcenter in the seventh frame. Stennett then tripled to right in the eighth frame, as Cubs' rightfielder Champ Summers dove for the ball and it bounced past him. Murtaugh sent in Willie Randolph to pinchrun for Rennie after the final hit. Amazingly, he failed to hit for the cycle. But no one will ever forget his performance.

Incredibly, Rennie Stennett became the fourth hitter, and second Pirate, in major league history who hit safely two times in an inning twice in a game. The others who accomplished that feat included Pirate Max Carey in 1925, John Hodapp of the Indians in 1928 and Sherman Lollar of the White Sox in 1955.

What people don't know is that Rennie Stennett asked Tony Bartirome, the trainer, to talk to Manager Danny Murtaugh to take him out of the game after his first four safeties due to his ankle problems. Murtaugh, however, replied, "No, let him bat until he makes an out." Tony Bartirome later told Rennie that if it wasn't for Murtaugh, he wouldn't have gotten the record.

John Candelaria got the victory against Rick Reuschel and the Pirates reduced their magic number to seven.

Tony Bartirome

For the record, the 22-run whitewashing eclipsed the mark set by the 1901 Detroit Tigers, who blitzed the Indians 21-0, and the 1939 New York Yankees, who defeated the Philadelphia Athletics by the same score.

Other interesting facts about the game included Dave Parker making two outs in the nine-run first inning, the Pirates collecting nineteen singles in the twenty-four hit attack, and Richie Hebner and Dave Parker clubbing the only two homers in the contest. Parker also picked up five rbi while Stargell and Taveras each collected three safeties. Every starter hit safely, drove in at least one run and scored at least one tally.

Naturally, the Pirates could feel the momentum growing to get their fifth division title in six years.

The next day they reduced their magic number even further with a 9-1 victory in Veteran's Stadium against the Phillies. Bruce Kison evened his record at 11-11 and the Pirates now owned an 87-64 record.

Steve Carlton defeated the Pirates by a 4-1 mark the following day, outhurling Dock Ellis.

Then it was time for the Pirates to return to Three Rivers again. Ken Brett triumphed over the Cardinals by a 7-1 count on September 19th. Then the Cardinals defeated the Pirates 8-2 the next day. Jerry Reuss then picked up his 17th win on September 21st against the Cardinals by a 5-3 margin and things looked good for the Pirates.

The Phillies then came to town and the Pirates celebrated by clinching their fifth division title on Monday, September 22nd, in a 11-3 victory. Bruce Kison got his twelfth victory and Kent Tekulve got the save. So the Pirates clinched the division with their 90th victory and owned an overall mark of 90-66. Now they could coast the rest of the way and get ready for the NLCS.

Bob Moose defeated Steve Carlton the next day in a 3-1 triumph for the team's 91st victory.

Then, in a battle of Larrys, Christenson defeated Demery by an 8-1 margin on September 24th.

The Pirates would close out the regular season on the road against the Cardinals. Bob Forsch defeated Jim Rooker in the first game by a 1-0 score. Jerry Reuss then got his 18th victory of the season in a 4-2 victory over Lynn McGlothen. Then the Pirates lost their last game of the regular season by a 6-2 count as Ron Reed defeated John Candelaria. Pittsburgh finished with a 92-69 record.

For the third time in six years, the Pirates and Reds would meet in the NLCS.

1975 FINAL LEAGUE STATISTICS

CLUB BATTING

Club	AVE.	AB	R	H	2B	3B	HR	RBI	SB	CS	E
St.L.	.273	5597	662	1527	239	46	81	619	116	49	171
Cin.	.271	5581	840	1515	278	37	124	779	168	36	102
Phil.	.269	5592	735	1506	283	42	125	687	126	57	152
Pitt.	.263	5489	712	1444	255	47	138	669	49	28	151
Chi.	.259	5470	712	1419	229	41	95	645	67	55	179
S.F.	.259	5447	659	1412	235	45	84	606	99	47	146
N.Y.	.256	5587	646	1430	217	34	101	604	32	26	151
Hous.	.254	5515	664	1401	218	54	84	606	133	62	137
L.A.	.248	5453	648	1355	217	31	118	606	138	52	127
Mtl.	.244	5518	601	1346	216	31	98	542	108	58	180
Atl.	.244	5424	583	1323	179	28	107	541	55	38	175
S.D.	.244	5429	552	1324	215	22	78	505	85	50	188
TOTALS	.257	66102	8014	17002	2781	458	1233	7409	1176	558	1859

AWARDED FIRST BASE ON INTERFERENCE: Brock, St.L. 2 (Johnson, Carter); Luzinski, Phil. 2 (Simmons 2); Phillips, N.Y. 2 (May, Foote); Torres, S.D. 2 (Hosley, May); Bench, Cin. (Foote); Bowa, Phil. (Swisher); Capra, Atl. (Boone); Hebner, Pitt. (Boone); Hundley, S.D. (Simmons); Hutton, Phil. (Simmons); May, Hou. (Correll); Perez, Atl. (Simmons).

CLUB PITCHING

Club	ERA	CG	SV	SHO	IP	H	R	ER	HR	BB	HB	SO
L.A.	2.92	51	21	18	1469.2	1215	534	477	104	448	28	894
Pitt.	3.01	43	31	14	1437.1	1302	565	480	79	551	20	768
Cin.	3.37	22	50	8	1459.0	1422	586	546	112	487	29	663
N.Y.	3.39	40	31	14	1466.0	1344	625	552	99	580	24	989
S.D.	3.48	40	20	12	1463.1	1494	683	566	99	521	24	713
St.L.	3.57	33	36	13	1454.2	1452	689	577	98	571	24	824
Mtl.	3.72	30	25	12	1480.0	1448	690	612	102	665	37	831
S.F.	3.74	37	24	9	1432.2	1406	671	595	92	612	38	856
Phil.	3.82	33	30	11	1455.0	1353	694	618	111	546	25	897
Atl.	3.91	32	24	4	1430.0	1543	739	622	101	519	44	669
Hous.	4.04	39	25	6	1458.1	1436	711	654	106	679	34	839
Chi.	4.49	27	33	8	1444.1	1587	827	721	130	551	40	850
TOTALS	3.62	427	350	129	17450.1	17002	8014	7020	1233	6730	367	9793

NOTE: Total earned runs for several clubs do not agree with composite total of respective club's pitchers due to provisions of Scoring Rule Section 10:18(i). The following differences are to be noted: Atlanta pitchers add to 624; Chicago 732; Houston 656; Montreal 614; Pittsburgh 482; St. Louis 578; San Diego 570.

1975 STANDINGS

Eastern Division

Club	W	L	Pct.	GB	Pitt.	Phil.	N.Y.	Stl.	Chi.	Mtl.	Atl.	Cin.	Hou.	L.A.	S.D.	S.F.	East W-L	West W-L
Pitt.	92	69	.571	–	–	7	13	10	12	11	8	6	5	7	8	5	53-37	39-32
Phil.	86	76	.531	6½	11	–	11	10	6	11	7	5	6	5	7	7	49-41	37-35
N.Y.	82	80	.506	10½	5	7	–	9	11	8	8	4	8	6	8	8	40-50	42-30
St.L.	82	80	.506	10½	8	8	9	–	7	7	9	4	8	7	8	7	39-51	43-29
Chi.	75	87	.463	17½	6	12	7	11	–	9	7	1	7	5	6	5	45-45	30-42
Mtl.	75	87	.463	17½	7	7	10	11	9	–	4	4	4	7	7	5	44-46	31-41

Western Division

Club	W	L	Pct.	GB	Cin.	L.A.	S.F.	S.D.	Atl.	Hou.	Chi.	Mtl.	N.Y.	Phil.	Pitt.	Stl.	West W-L	East W-L
Cin.	108	54	.667	–	–	8	13	11	15	13	11	8	8	7	6	8	60-30	48-24
L.A.	88	74	.543	20	10	–	10	11	10	12	7	5	6	7	5	5	53-37	35-37
S.F.	80	81	.497	27½	5	8	–	10	9	13	7	7	4	5	7	5	45-44	35-37
S.D.	71	91	.438	37	7	7	8	–	11	9	7	5	4	5	4	4	42-48	29-43
Atl.	67	94	.416	40½	3	8	8	7	–	12	5	8	4	5	4	3	38-51	29-43
Hous.	64	97	.398	43½	5	6	5	9	6	–	5	8	4	6	6	4	31-59	33-38

TIES: Houston at St. Louis (3-3), August 25 (10 innings)
CHAMPIONSHIP SERIES: Cincinnati defeated Pittsburgh 3 games to 0.

1975 PITTSBURGH FINAL STATISTICS

Batting—Fielding

Player	AVE.	G	AB	R	H	2B	3B	HR	RBI	SH-SF	BB-I	HB	SO	SB-CS	GDP	PO	A	E
Brett	.231	26	52	5	12	4	0	1	4	1-0	1-0	0	7	0-0	1	13	18	1
Candelaria	.140	18	43	2	6	0	0	0	2	0-0	3-0	0	12	0-0	0	3	13	4
Demery	.125	49	24	3	3	0	1	0	0	2-0	4-0	0	10	0-0	0	7	13	1
Dilone	.000	18	6	8	0	0	0	0	0	0-0	0-0	0	1	2-2	0	3	0	0
Dyer	.227	48	132	8	30	5	2	3	16	1-0	6-0	1	22	0-0	4	187	14	2
Ellis	.111	30	36	3	4	1	0	0	1	7-0	5-0	0	8	0-0	1	8	16	2
Giusti	.300	61	10	2	3	0	0	0	1	4-0	1-0	0	2	0-0	0	4	17	3
Hebner	.246	128	472	65	116	16	4	15	57	3-5	43-6	10	48	0-1	7	86	244	19
Hernandez	.000	46	6	0	0	0	0	0	0	2-0	2-0	0	2	0-0	0	1	13	0
Howe	.171	63	146	13	25	9	0	1	10	1-0	15-3	0	15	1-0	5	19	89	7
Jones	.000	2	0	0	0	0	0	0	0	0-0	0-0	0	0	0-0	0	0	1	0
Kirkpatrick	.236	89	144	15	34	5	0	5	16	1-1	18-2	0	22	1-0	5	167	9	0
Kison	.119	35	59	4	7	0	0	0	3	10-0	2-0	0	29	1-0	0	11	39	1
McDowell	.000	14	8	0	0	0	0	0	0	0-0	0-0	0	5	0-0	0	1	5	0
Mendoza	.180	56	50	8	9	1	0	0	2	3-0	3-0	0	17	0-0	1	29	70	5
Minshall	.000	1	0	0	0	0	0	0	0	0-0	0-0	0	0	0-0	0	0	0	0
Moose	.167	23	18	1	3	0	0	0	0	2-0	1-0	0	8	0-0	2	6	16	1
Moreno	.167	6	6	1	1	0	0	0	0	0-0	1-0	0	1	1-0	0	0	0	1
Oliver	.280	155	628	90	176	39	8	18	84	0-8	25-3	5	73	4-2	19	409	6	5
Ott	.200	5	5	0	1	0	0	0	0	0-0	0-0	0	0	0-0	0	2	0	0
Parker	.308	148	558	75	172	35	10	25	101	0-1	38-4	5	89	8-6	18	311	7	9
Popovich	.200	25	40	5	8	1	0	0	1	0-0	3-0	1	2	0-0	0	17	21	1
Randolph	.164	30	61	9	10	1	0	0	3	1-1	7-1	0	6	1-0	3	34	45	6
Reuss	.197	32	71	6	14	2	0	0	2	10-0	5-0	0	27	0-0	0	6	48	0
Reynolds	.224	31	76	8	17	3	0	0	4	0-0	3-1	0	5	0-1	1	43	82	4
Robertson	.274	75	124	17	34	4	0	6	18	0-3	23-0	2	25	0-0	0	209	18	1
Robinson	.280	92	200	26	56	12	2	6	33	3-3	11-4	0	36	3-1	6	107	3	1
Rooker	.095	28	63	4	6	0	0	0	2	9-0	3-0	0	20	0-0	1	10	32	4
Sanguillen	.328	133	481	60	158	24	4	9	58	2-3	48-15	3	31	5-4	12	650	53	9
Stargell	.295	124	461	71	136	32	2	22	90	0-4	58-6	3	109	0-0	9	1121	54	10
Stennett	.286	148	616	89	176	25	7	7	62	6-5	33-1	4	42	5-4	15	379	463	18
Taveras	.212	134	378	44	80	9	4	0	23	8-2	37-0	2	42	17-6	2	200	369	28
Tekulve	.091	34	11	1	1	0	0	0	1	0-0	1-0	0	7	0-0	0	5	17	1
Zisk	.290	147	504	69	146	27	3	20	75	0-4	68-9	2	109	0-1	12	264	7	7
Totals	.263	161	5489	712	1444	255	47	138*	669	76-40	468-55	38*	832	49-28	124	4312	1802	151
Opponents	.243	161	5369	565	1302	209	41	79	523	93-36	551-102	20	768	81-34	119	–	–	133

Pitching

Player	W	L	ERA	G	GS	CG	GF	SV	SHO	IP	H	R	ER	HR	BB-I	HB	SO	WP	BK	BFP
Brett	9	5	3.36	23	16	4	8	0	1	118.0	110	47	44	10	43-5	2	47	5	1	492
Candelaria	8	6	2.75	18	18	4	4	0	1	120.2	95	47	37	8	36-9	2	95	1	0	497
Demery	7	5	2.90	45	8	1	24	4	0	114.2	95	40	37	7	43-6	3	59	3	0	468
Ellis	8	9	3.79	27	24	5	6	0	2	140.0	163	69	59	9	43-9	3	69	0	2	621
Giusti	5	4	2.93	61	0	0	43	17	0	91.2	79	38	30	3	42-17	0	38	2	1	389
Hernandez	7	2	2.95	46	0	0	27	5	0	64.0	62	21	21	0	28-14	0	43	1	0	280
Jones	0	0	0.00	2	0	0	1	0	0	3.0	1	0	0	0	0-0	0	2	0	0	10
Kison	12	11	3.23	33	29	6	6	0	0	192.0	160	89	69	10	92-9	4	89	9	2	819
McDowell	2	1	2.83	14	1	0	4	0	0	34.2	30	11	11	0	20-3	0	29	1	2	149
Minshall	0	0	0.00	1	0	0	1	0	0	1.0	0	0	0	0	2-0	0	2	0	0	5
Moose	2	2	3.71	23	5	1	6	0	0	67.2	63	30	28	4	25-3	2	34	3	1	287
Reuss	18	11	2.54	32	32	15	15	0	6	237.1	224	73	67	10	78-8	0	131	4	1	984
Rooker	13	11	2.97	28	28	7	7	0	1	196.2	177	80	65	16	76-13	3	102	5	1	839
Tekulve	1	2	2.25	34	0	0	9	5	0	56.0	43	20	14	2	23-6	1	28	3	0	232
Totals	92	69	3.01	161	161	43	161	31	14#	1437.1	1302	565	480	79+	551-102	20	768	37	11	6072
Opponents	69	92	4.08	161	161	39	161	22	13	1427.2	1444	712	647	138	468-55	38	832	47	9	–

(*) Denotes League Leadership
(#) Combined Shutouts (3): Brett and Giusti – vs. St. L. 4/20 Brett, Hernandez and Giusti – vs. Chi. 7/7 Candelaria, Brett and Hernandez – vs. Chi. 9/16
(+) Pirate staff allowed 79 home runs for lowest total in league
Pirate team ERA total of 480 is 2 less than individual total under scoring rule 10:18

PITT. VS. EASTERN DIV.

	Home	Road	Total
Chi.	6-3	6-3	12-6
Mtl.	5-4	6-3	11-7
N.Y.	5-4	8-1	13-5
Phil.	6-3	1-8	7-11
St. L.	6-3	4-5	10-8
			53-37

PITT. VS. WESTERN DIV.

	Home	Road	Total
Atl.	4-2	4-2	8-4
Cin.	4-2	2-4	6-6
Hous.	4-1	1-5	5-6
L.A.	3-3	4-2	7-5
S.D.	5-1	3-3	8-4
S.F.	4-2	1-5	5-7
			39-32

John Candelaria #45

Game three 1975 NLCS

CINCINNATI	ab	r	h	bi	PITTSBURGH	ab	r	h	bi
Rose,3b	5	2	2	2	Stennett,2b	5	0	0	0
Morgan,2b	5	0	2	1	Hebner,3b	5	1	2	0
Bench,c	5	0	0	0	AOliver,cf	5	1	1	2
TPerez,1b	4	0	0	0	Stargell,1b	4	0	1	0
GFoster,lf	3	0	0	0	Randolph,2b	1	1	0	0
Concepcion,ss	4	1	1	1	DParker,rf	4	0	0	0
Griffey,rf	4	1	1	0	Zisk,lf	3	0	2	0
Geronimo,cf	4	0	0	0	Sanguillen,c	4	0	1	0
Nolan,p	2	0	0	0	Taveras,ss	1	0	0	0
CCarroll,p	0	0	0	0	Kirkptrck,ph	1	0	0	0
Rettmund,ph	0	1	0	0	Reynolds,ss	1	0	0	0
McEnany,p	0	0	0	0	Robertson,1b	0	0	0	0
Eastwick,p	0	0	0	0	Candelaria,p	3	0	0	0
Armbrister,ph	0	0	0	1	Giusti,p	0	0	0	0
Borbon,p	0	0	0	0	Dyer,ph	0	0	0	1
					Hernandez,p	0	0	0	0
					Tekulve,p	0	0	0	0
Total	36	5	6	5	Total	37	3	7	3

```
Cincinnati  ........................  010  000  020   2-5
Pittsburgh-  .......................  000  002  001   0-3
```

E—Reynolds, Sanguillen. LOB—Cincinnati 4, Pittsburgh 7. 2B—Morgan 2. HR—Concepcion (1), A. Oliver (1), Rose (1). SB—Bench. SF—Armbrister.

	IP	H	R	ER	BB	SO
Nolan	6	5	2	2	0	5
C. Carroll	1	0	0	0	1	1
McEnaney	1⅓	1	1	1	0	1
Eastwick (W,1-0)	⅔	1	0	0	2	0
Borbon	1	0	0	0	0	1
Candelaria	7⅔	3	3	3	2	14
Giusti	1⅓	0	0	0	0	1
Hernandez (L,0-1)	⅔	3	2	2	0	0
Tekulve	⅓	0	0	0	0	0

Save—Borbon (1). Balk—Hernandez. T—2:47. A—46,355.

WAS THE THIRD TIME A CHARM AGAINST THE CINCINNATI REDS?

For the third time in six years, the Pirates and Reds would meet in the NLCS. In 1970, the Reds easily beat the Pirates in three straight, as Cincinnati clearly stood as a superior squad. Then, when the two teams met again in 1972, most baseball observers considered the Pirates the superior team but Pittsburgh lost on that famous wild pitch. Now came 1975, and the Reds had an amazing season as they finished with an 108-54 mark while the Pirates sported a 92-69 record. This time the Reds clearly had the statistical advantage as well as the first two games at home in Riverfront.

Pittsburgh's Pirates won the NL Eastern Division by 6.5 games over the Philadelphia Phillies as they stayed in first place most of the season. Their offensive attack featured two .300 hitters in the form of Manny Sanguillen(.328) and Dave Parker(.308). Parker also lead the team with 101 rbi and the NL in slugging percentage with a .541 mark. The rest of the "Lumber Company", Richie Zisk, Willie Stargell, Rennie Stennett, Al Oliver and Bill Robinson, all checked in with averages of .280 or better. Jerry Reuss and Jim

Rooker had good seasons on the mound with records of 18-11 and 15-11, while John Candelaria showed great promise as a rookie hurler. Dave Giusti, Kent Tekulve and Ramon Hernandez held the bullpen together.

Yet Cincinnati's Reds looked twice as good. They had four .300 hitters in Joe Morgan, Pete Rose, Ken Griffey and George Foster. Tony Perez and Johnny Bench both collected 100 rbi. On top of that, Bench, Perez and Foster all had 20 or more homers. That power enabled the Reds to go from a 20-20 record on May 21st, five games behind the Dodgers, to a 108-54 mark at the end of the season, which was twenty games in front of Los Angeles. At one point, they won forty-one of fifty contests.

So the Pirates went into this NLCS as a clear underdog. Yet they felt confident.

In the first game of the NLCS, Don Gullett faced Jerry Reuss before 54,633 fans at Riverfront. The Reds triumphed by an 8-3 score as pitcher Don Gullett hit a homerun and the Reds' baserunners stole five bases. Murtaugh used five pitchers in the game as Reuss got knocked out after two innings. Cincinnati outhit the Pirates 11-8 and clearly showed their superiority.

Then, in the second game of the NLCS, Fred Norman defeated Jim Rooker by a 6-1 count as the Reds outhit the Buccos with 12 safeties to the Buccos 5. Murtaugh used four hurlers in this contest, as Rooker, Tekulve, Brett, and Kison all contributed. Tony Perez hit a homerun in this game and Cincinnati looked unbeatable at this point. The Reds added five more steals.

Rookie John Candelaria put forth an incredible effort in the third game of the NLCS at Three Rivers Stadium, as he mowed down 14 Cincinnati hitters on strikeouts. Despite getting those 14 k's in 7 2/3 innings of work, Pete Rose hit an eighth-inning homerun to knock out the rookie lefthander. Al Oliver and Dave Concepcion also hit big homers. Giusti, Hernandez and Tekulve all saw action in relief. Rawley Eastwick got the victory and Pedro Borbon got the save while Ramon Hernandez got credit for the loss.

Although the Pirates lost to the Reds for the third time in the '70's, they couldn't hang their heads. After all, Cincinnati's Big Red Machine stood as the most explosive team since the Yankees of the 1950's.

Looking back over the statistics for the NLCS, the Reds totally dominated. Cincinnati had a .284 batting average for the series while the Pirates hit .198. Then, as far as pitching went, the Pirates had a 6.58 era to the Reds' 2.25. The Bucco hitters had only one homer and seven rbi while The Big Red Machine had four homers and eighteen rbi. So it didn't take a genius to figure out the reasons for the loss.

The Pirates could feel very positive about their season for many reasons. They had become a legitimate contender again after having just won their fifth division title in six campaigns. Only the Oakland A's could match them with their success.

Longtime Pirate employee Sally O'Leary remembers, "In 1974 and 1975 we were still NL Eastern Division Champs but just couldn't handle the Dodgers and Reds. It's so disappointing when you get that far- and all of a sudden it's over! But there were many great games and lots of nice memories anyway!"

That was so true. The Pirates had a lot of great games, a lot of good statistics and many nice memories.

Statistically speaking, the Pirates' record was a stellar one. They had a 52-28 mark at

Dave Parker   **#39**

Three Rivers and a 40-41 record. Looking back over the stat sheets, you will notice that they were 34-39 against lefthanders, 58-40 against righthanders, 61-42 at night, 31-27 in day games, 17-20 in one-run contests, 4-7 in extra-innings, 6-4-3 in doubleheaders, had 42 come-from-behind wins and triumphed 20 times in their last at bat.

Offensively, the Pirates had five primary rbi producers but only two .300 hitters. Dave Parker lead the way with 25 homers, 101 rbi, a .308 batting average and

a .541 slugging percentage. Stargell sported a .295 average with 22 homers and 90 rbi. Richie Zisk managed to hit .290 with 20 roundtrippers and 75 rbi. Al Oliver checked in with a .280 average while hitting 18 homers and driving in 84. Richie Hebner had a subpar .246 average but still had 15 circuit clouts and 57 rbi.

Yet the positive side of the offense focused on the Pirates having a .263 team batting average, good for fourth in the NL, while leading the loop in homers with 138.

The hurling also sparkled in 1975 as the Pirates finished second in the National League with a 3.01 team era. They yielded the fewest homers with only 79 while also giving up the second fewest earned runs(480) and runs(565). Only the Los Angeles Dodgers, a team traditionally known for hurling, had better pitching stats.

Jerry Reuss finished among the top four hurlers in the NL, as he tied for second in the loop with six shutouts, tied for third with fifteen complete games, and placed fourth best in the senior circuit with a 2.54 era and eighteen wins. He also had a .197 batting average with 14 hits. Besides that, he got to start the All-Star Game.

Jim Rooker finished with a 13-11 mark and placed eighth in the National League with a 2.97 era. Bruce Kison also had a good season with a 12-11 record and a 3.23 era. Ken Brett had a 9-5 mark while also sporting a .231 batting average.

The Pirates also gained stability. Stennett and Taveras really worked well together as a double-play combo. Zisk and Parker both got better with another season of work. Basically, the Buccos still had the strong foundation of strong hitting, pitching and defense that made them one of the top teams in the whole decade.

Pirate fans and players felt good about their team's chances to stay in contention for years to come.

But the front office still felt some tweaking needed to be done.

Doc Ellis   **#17**

On December 11, 1975, Joe L. Brown sent Willie Randolph, Ken Brett and Dock Ellis to the New York Yankees for pitcher Doc Medich, who had won 49 games in three seasons. They felt they needed to get Medich to improve the righthanded portion of the staff. Little did they know that Randolph would anchor the Yankee infield for a decade.

But the biggest change came up in the broadcast booth as KDKA management fired Bob Prince and Nellie King after several great years. Everyone was shocked. "The Gunner" had served the Pirates for 25 years with his famous phrases such as "Homerun in an elevator shaft," "Hoover," "Bug on the rug," and "We had 'em all the way." Milo Hamilton and Lanny Frattare would take over in the booth.

Most Pirate fans couldn't believe it and showed their support with a rally downtown that over 10,000 attended.

Was it only a coincidence that the Pirates would not win the divisional title for three more years? Pirate baseball would never be the same.

SPREAD SOME CHICKEN ON THE HILL WITH WILL

Perhaps no slugger in history generated the same enthusiasm as Willie did in Pittsburgh when Bob Prince used to exhort him,"Spread some chicken on the hill with Will," a phrase that meant that if Stargell would hit a homer, everyone who was in his chicken restaurant in the Hill District of Pittsburgh would get free fowl. Whenever Stargell would connect, Prince would automatically cheer him on with that famous exhortation. Everyone in Pittsburgh would join along with that exhortation, even to the point of using it in local pickup baseball games in the old neighborhood.

I'll never forget how all the neighborhood kids would imitate the famous windmill swing in those famous games of homerun derby.

I remember countless times when he won games in the bottom of the ninth inning at Three Rivers Stadium after Bob Prince's exhortation for a "bloop and a blast," which meant that someone, often Clemente or someone else in the order, would get on with a bunt or some other type of single and then Stargell would uncork his windmill to send one of the opposing pitcher's deliveries into orbit as the Pirate fans erupted in pandemonium.

Willie Stargell's windmill truly dominated the National League like few others. That motion scared opposing hurlers. Even Don Sutton admitted that he sometimes held the ball a little longer hoping that Willie would just go away.

Willie's statistics for the '70's transcend all the other great hitters of that era- Reggie Jackson, Johnny Bench, Lee May and Billy Williams. He lead all major league hitters in the decade of the '70's with 296 roundtrippers and also eclipsed all sluggers with 1,100 rbi in the same period. Reggie Jackson and Johnny Bench finished close to Stargell with 292 and 290 homers, respectively. In the rbi department, Bench finished with 1,013 and Tony Perez had 954. So Stargell had one of the more impressive decades in history.

Who will ever forget his incredible years of 1971 and 1973, when he lead the NL with 48 homers and 44, respectively. He also hit in the .290's. Both years he could have won the MVP Award, especially in '73 when he lead both leagues in six different offensive categories- homers, rbi, doubles, extra-basehits, slugging and game-winning hits. Yet he wouldn't win that award until 1979, when "The Family" all came together.

Something about Stargell captivated fans. He had a certain quality that other sluggers of his era such as Aaron and Mays didn't possess. It was a rythmn that gave him a certain smoothness as a slugger. He just looked better hitting a homerun than other sluggers.

And boy could he drive that ball. He hit some of the most impressive shots in the history of baseball, having hit seven balls out of Forbes Field, two out of Dodger Stadium and three into the upper deck at Three Rivers Stadium. Someone once said that if you measured all of Stargell's shots and compared the distance of his 475 roundtrippers to Ruth's 714 or Aaron's 755, his balls would have traveled much farther. "Stargellic" should be an adjective to describe an impressive homer.

The honors went on and on for Stargell.

In 1982, in Stargell's last season with the team as an active player, the Pirates retired his number in a special emotional ceremony at Three Rivers Stadium, the facility in which he homered 147 times in his career, three of the upper deck variety.

He became only the 17th player in history to enter Cooperstown's doors in his first year of eligibility when he got inducted in 1988. That shows what a legend he was.

Willie got selected to seven all-star teams.

And he also performed in the clutch with seven postseason homers. Who will forget his incredible postseason in 1979 when he won the MVP of both the NLCS and the World Series with clutch homers? His homer against Scott McGregor with Bill Robinson on base in Game Seven of the 1979 World Series sent Pittsburgh into a hysterical celebration.

Yet people forget about what a great leftfielder he was! His arm, although many people didn't often notice it with Clemente in the same outfield, cut down many a baserunner on the basepaths. Who will ever forget his throw to Manny Sanguillen to cut down Davey Johnson at the plate in Game Two of the 1971 World Series?

He played very well defensively at first base as well. Willie actually played 1293 games in the outfield and 848 at first base.

The official stats show 475 homers and 1540 rbi in a 20-year career.

Yet it's the legend of the windmill swing that will live on for years. Stargell drove baseballs consistently further than any slugger and that includes Babe Ruth, "Stretch" McCovey, Hank Aaron, Willie Mays or Mickey Mantle.

Those other sluggers clubbed homers. Wilver Dornell Stargell did more than that. Willie spread chicken on the hill!

Willie Stargell's Hall of Fame Plaque
Courtesy National Baseball Hall of Fame and Museum

THE GUTS OF A CHAMPION

What do we mean by a champion, especially in the City of Champions? One definition stands as someone who exhibits certain characteristics to reach excellence by paying attention to the details. It's more than being good. Greatness comes from exhibiting those characteristics over a long period of time, which yields success.

Yet what characterizes a champion? Many ingredients come together to form a baseball champion like the Pirates, including courage, daring aggressiveness, dedication, concentration, poise, confidence, tenacity and sportsmanship. Mix all these ingredients together in their proper combination and you will get a champion.

Examples of these qualities abounded in the playing careers of the Pirates who played in the mustard hats.

Certainly, courage applied to Rennie Stennett of these Pirates. During one game in the 1974 campaign in the ninth inning against the Dodgers in a crucial contest, reliever Dave Giusti came on to retire Los Angeles. The first out was on the board. Anything other than a doubleplay would tie the game. The Buccos had to get a double dip against Bill Buckner, one of the more swift runners in the league. On a slow roller to short, Stennett grabbed the ball, stepped on second and relayed it to first to get Buckner by a half-step and preserve the victory. Rennie hung in there in the ninth with the runner bearing down on him. Later in his career, he came back to play after a terrible ankle injury. His career exemplified courage.

Yet daring aggressiveness also makes or breaks the champion, as being too conservative often squelches key opportunities. Al Oliver illustrated this principle beautifully in the last game of the 1974 campaign in the bottom of the tenth inning when he hit what appeared to be a double into leftfield but then wouldn't let anything stop him from getting to third base for the triple. Many runners would not have tried for third base in that situation. But Oliver knew how important it would be to get to third and win that division-clinching game. He then scored the division-winning run soon after that and the Pirates won their fourth division title.

Champions also need dedication, whether a person starts or serves as a utility man. Pirate catcher Mike Ryan, when he played with the Pirates, exhibited this on a daily basis. Although he knew he wouldn't play on a regular basis with all-star Manny Sanguillen behind the plate for the Pirates, he stayed ready and helped other players stay sharp. The Pirates got him because of his strong arm and quick release and he also served as the utility catcher for the Phillies for four seasons. Yet he also played on a regular basis with Philadelphia in 1969 and tied Randy Hundley for the league lead in assists among catchers with 79. So he knew how to stay dedicated, whether as a starter or as a backup.

Furthermore, don't forget the concentration that many of the Pirates exhibited, none more than Al Oliver. People who saw Al bat will never forget how he truly focused in with his gameface when he came to the plate against the great pitchers of his day, whether Bob Gibson, Tom Seaver or Don Sutton. That concentration allowed him to collect 2,743 hits in his career to go with a .303 lifetime batting average. Tom Seaver actually admitted that Al Oliver was the toughest out in the Pirate lineup.

No Pirate displayed championship poise better than Willie Stargell, who often asserted,"I never get too high after a win and never too low after a loss." His even disposition gave him the ability to deal with 162 games. That poise stands as the quality that doesn't allow you to lose control, whether getting too positive in a winning situation or too negative in a losing situation. That's why many athletes burn out in the midst of a 162-game season. Stargell competed in the major leagues for 20 years.

Confidence also plays a key part in the guts of a champion and no one exemplified that better than Dave Giusti, the famous relief pitcher who finished fourth in saves in the '70's with 140. He had his ups and downs, as all relievers do. To illustrate, he got all the key saves in the postseason in '71 and also won Fireman of the Year. Then, in 1972, with the NL pennant on the line, he gave up the game-tying homer to Johnny Bench in the bottom of the ninth. But he didn't let that ruin him, as many people would. He came back to make the All-Star Game in 1973 and hurled for a few more years after that. That confidence must stay with you, for champions get tested in the cauldron of competition.

The whole team, especially the 1974 squad, showed everyone how vital tenacity stands in the life of a champion. As Al Oliver so aptly put it, "The writers gave up on us and so did the fans. But we didn't give up on ourselves." That allowed them to clinch the division in the bottom of the tenth inning of game number 162 despite having a subpar year.

Yet, in the midst of all this serious competition, never lose the sense of sportsmanship, respect for your opponent whether you win or lose. The Pirates of 1972 obviously illustrated that principle in a way that few baseball teams ever have or will. Some of the Pirates actually went to the Red clubhouse and had the graciousness to congratulate them after that NLCS. Because most of the core group of players on that 1972 team still remained on the roster in the last two division titles, you can bet that they practiced good sportsmanship.

But that sportsmanship even overflowed into off the field activities as well.

Champions reach out to the unfortunate and the needy, to spread that positive feeling about winning to other people's lives, and the Pirates certainly did that. Manny Sanguillen taught the Bible and sports to youngsters in Pan-American missions and reached out to those in the Toner Institute in Mount Lebanon. Al Oliver served in the Big Brothers and Sisters Program. Steve Blass served with the Muscular Dystrophy Association. Willie Stargell helped with Sickle Cell Research with his bowling tournament and in other ways. Many other players involved themselves in tangible outreach to the community.

So the Pirates truly had the guts of a champion both on and off the field.

Courtesy Pittsburgh Pirates

HANG IN THERE AND GET IT TOGETHER!

Baseball, more than any other sport, symbolizes life. Players compete on an everyday basis and have very few offdays. Just as in life, players can not get too high or too low. For that very reason it's critical for them to hang in there.

The Pirates of the early '70's understood how to hang in there. To win five division titles in six years, you have to hang in there. After all, the Pirates coasted to some of their division titles, yet they clinched one title on the last day of the season and then lost another one at the end of the season. So they had to learn how to deal with the ups and the downs.

Stargell certainly had a steadying influence with his philosophy of not getting too high or too low.

Manny Sanguillen and Jose Pagan, two of the Christians associated with the team, also contributed positively.

Gale Sayers, HOF running back with the Chicago Bears, propagated one of those important philosophies in I AM THIRD, when he asserted, "The Lord is first, my friends are second and I am third." That theme certainly touched a lot of people in the athletic world, especially with the release of the movie BRIAN'S SONG.

Many people, especially in athletics, have success, money, fame, sex or drugs as their god instead of God. Many fans even lose perspective and allow the fortunes of their favorite team or player to dominate their whole life. Having God first truly allows you to get it together.

Former NFL All-Pro Bill Glass often preaches to athletes and those connected with the sports world and he affirmed,"The greatest cause the world has ever known is the cause of Jesus Christ."

Los Angeles Dodger pitcher Geoff Zahn, himself a member of the 1974 team that played the Pirates in the NLCS, declared after one of Glass's messages in 1974,"Three years ago I came to know the Lord. It's exciting to be a Christian in baseball."

Former major league outfielder Albie Pearson, who later became a pastor in California, cautioned, however,"For a long time I was a plastic Christian. The only time I called on God was when I was 0 for 20 at bat. I've asked God to set me free and He has."

Glass asks listeners to stand openly for Jesus and not to become "gutless wonders."

"Like in football," he warned, "If you take a casual stance, you'll be knocked on your casual can."

Glass doesn't hold anything back in his messages and added,"You've seen the loser's limp on television. The defensive back gets beat on a play and 50 million people watch him limp to the bench. Christians do the same thing when they make excuses on why they aren't serving the Lord effectively."

Additionally, Bill Glass acknowledges,"Jesus is a specialist at forgiving great sinners. Every loser can become a winner. That's what God has in mind."

Manny Sanguillen and Jose Pagan both know what Glass means.

Sanguillen got to the major leagues because of a life-changing encounter "when he met Jesus Christ."

In Colon, Panama, Sanguillen lived in poverty and was the son of an alcoholic father. He started work at thirteen, often working from dawn to dusk for thirty-five cents an hour. Often, when he wasn't sleeping or working, he roamed the streets looking for fights, romancing, gambling or drinking.

Then he met a foreigner on a street corner who told him,"You can have a new life and be a new person." That Canadian missionary named Elmer Fehr encouraged him,"Turn to Jesus Christ who died for your sins. Believe in Him and become a new person."

Manny and others hung around him to get to know him personally.

Mr. Fehr invited Manny and three other boys to come to his house the next day. That meeting would change Sanguillen's life.

At the meeting, the preacher asked if Manny and the other boys would help him organize a baseball team. Sanguillen agreed to help, despite the fact that he had only played basketball and soccer.

The team they put together did so well that they competed in Panama City.

Interestingly enough, the missionary and his wife considered Manny almost a part of the family. On offnights, the three of them would spend long evenings discussing the Bible. Sanguillen really appreciated the love and peace he experienced in their home. One night he prayed to receive Christ as his Lord and Savior.

A short time later, Manny considered going to seminary in Mexico City when a scout from the Pittsburgh Pirates watched him play in Panama City. That scout, a man named Howie Haak, offered him a contract. Sanguillen talked it over with his spiritual mentor and that missionary told him that he might reach more people with the gospel as a major league baseball player than as a preacher. Manny went to Florida for spring training in 1965 and six years later he appeared in the World Series.

Manny declared,"My life belongs to God one hundred percent. We go up and down in baseball but God never changes."

Jose Pagan, a player with the Pirates until 1972 and a coach in '74 and '75, also knows that same peace. He even joined the Fellowship of Christian Athletes.

That relationship with Christ enables everyone to hang in there and get it together.

Manny Sanguillen   **#35**

BIBLIOGRAPHY

Adelman, Bob and Hall, Susan. OUT OF LEFTFIELD: WILLIE STARGELL AND THE PITTSBURGH PIRATES. New York: Two Continents Publishing Group, 1976..

Angell, Roger. FIVE SEASONS: A BASEBALL COMPANION. New York: Simon and Schuster, 1977.

Chadys, Joel; Guilfoile, Bill and O'Leary, Sally. PITTSBURGH PIRATES OFFICIAL 1974 AND 1975 YEARBOOKS and 1975 MEDIA GUIDE. Pittsburgh: Pittsburgh Pirates.

Dickson, Paul. THE NEW DICKSON BASEBALL DICTIONARY. Boston: Harcourt Brace and Company, 1999.

Hefley, James C. RUNNING WITH GOD. New York: Avon Books, 1975.

Pepe, Phil. TALKING BASEBALL-AN ORAL HISTORY OF BASEBALL IN THE 1970's.
New York: Ballantine Books, 1998.

Smizik, Bob. THE PITTSBURGH PIRATES: AN ILLUSTRATED HISTORY. Edited by Geraldo Astor. New York: Walker and Company, 1990.

Trdinich, Jim. PITTSBURGH PIRATES 2000 AND 2002 MEDIA GUIDES. Pittsburgh.

Wolff, Rick. THE BASEBALL ENCYCLOPEDIA. New York: Macmillan Publishing Company, 1993.

Internet: BaseballLibrary.com; Baseball-Almanac.com

Three Rivers that Spawned The City of Champions

By Gregory S. Spalding

The fact that it was the first ballpark I went to as a young boy will always hold a special place in my heart. Although we will all look forward to the beautiful view of the Pittsburgh skyline at PNC Park, Three Rivers Stadium's circular construction allowed baseball fans to escape to another world for a few hours. It was a baseball escape for a few hours." *Tim DeBacco, Pirates Public Address Announcer.*

"I didn't think the closing was going to be that big a deal. But the closer it got the more I realized how much I was going to miss it. I was looking around that place and memories were popping up in my head everywhere I looked." *John Wehner, Pittsburgh Pirates Third Baseman.*

"I'll never forget the celebration of the anniversary of the first Super Bowl team. Dallas Cowboy fans go 'Yeah!' But Steeler fans roar." *Jon Kolb, former Pittsburgh Steeler offensive tackle ('69-'81) and coach.*

"My greatest memory was the first time I walked into that stadium. I said to myself, 'Look at this.' I looked around and the place was filled with banners. I saw Lambert's Lunatics and Gerela's Gorillas. I said to myself. 'You're part of something here.' *"Robin Cole, former Pittsburgh Steeler linebacker ('77-'87)*

"I know a lot of people say, 'It's only a building.' Well, it is. But there are alot of memories for me there, both through work and as a fan of the Pirates and Steelers." *Tim Friday, Three Rivers Stadium Usher.*

Three Rivers that Spawned
The City of Champions

By Gregory S. Spalding

- Over 150 photos-most of them of the unique variety

- All-time Three Rivers Stadium Pirate and Steeler teams

- The 31 most significant games

- The 27 playoff teams

- Many other notable moments

- Trivia, Box scores and Stats

- Unique photos and descriptions of the Implosion and the last games

REMEMBER THE 1994 ALL-STAR WEEK?

SHINE! ALL-STARS, SHINE! WILL HELP YOU NEVER FORGET!

YOU'LL ENJOY THE FOLLOWING IN THE 8 1/2 X 11 COMPENDIUM:

- OVER 125 PHOTOS COVERING EVERY ALL-STAR WEEK EVENT

- BOULEVARD OF THE ALL-STARS PHOTO SEGMENT

- TRIVIA AND STATS ABOUT THE PIRATES AND THE ALL-STAR GAME

- CLEMENTE STATUE DEDICATION PHOTOS

- PICTURES OF THE WORKOUT DAY, WHICH INCLUDED THE HEROES GAME AND HOMERUN DERBY

- PICTURES AND STATS FROM THE 1994 ALL-STAR GAME

- HOW TO BE AN ALL-STAR IN THE GAME OF LIFE WITH FEATURES ABOUT JAY BELL AND ANDY VAN SLYKE

- MISCELLANEOUS PHOTOS OF ALL-STAR WEEK

Send me _____ copies of SHINE! ALL-STARS, SHINE! for $20 plus $2 postage and handling.

NAME _____

ADDRESS _____

PHONE _____

Check or money order in the amount of _____ made out to City of Champions Publishing Company enclosed. Send to : City of Champions Publishing Company, Box 17276, Pgh, Pa 15235.

412-594-4827

(More info on other side)

From the All-Star Game's inception, Pittsburgh, the Pirates and the two stadiums participated mightily in the mid-summer classic's history. Forbes Field hosted two games and Three Rivers did the same. Sixty-six Pirates suited up for the National League over the years.

At a SABR(Society for American Baseball Research) meeting at Three Rivers Stadium in December, Pirate Marketing Vice President Steve Greenberg asserted(about the '94 All-Star Game),"It was great to see what baseball means to Pittsburgh. The All-Star week was such a high. Pittsburgh shined for five days."

Naturally, Greg focused much of his photos on those five days that Pittsburgh shined in '94, including events such as the Clemente Statue dedication, the Workout Day, the Fanfest, and the All-Star Game itself. Yet you will also notice much space devoted to previous all-star history.

Shine! All-Stars, Shine! celebrates the All-Star tradition of the Pirates, the city of Pittsburgh and the two stadiums in word and picture. Enjoy reliving the nostalgic moments of the wonderful mid-summer classics.

Author-Photographer Greg Spalding , pictured above promoting his *Sailing the Three Rivers to the Title*(the only book ever written about the '71 Pirates) at a Bucco appreciation event sponsored by WCNS radio, owns his home-based City of Champions Publishing Company, a literature distribution concern and desktop publishing entity. Additionally, he teaches Spanish, coaches and plays basketball, has served as a missionary and enjoys his membership in SABR. He majored in business/communications at Grove City College.

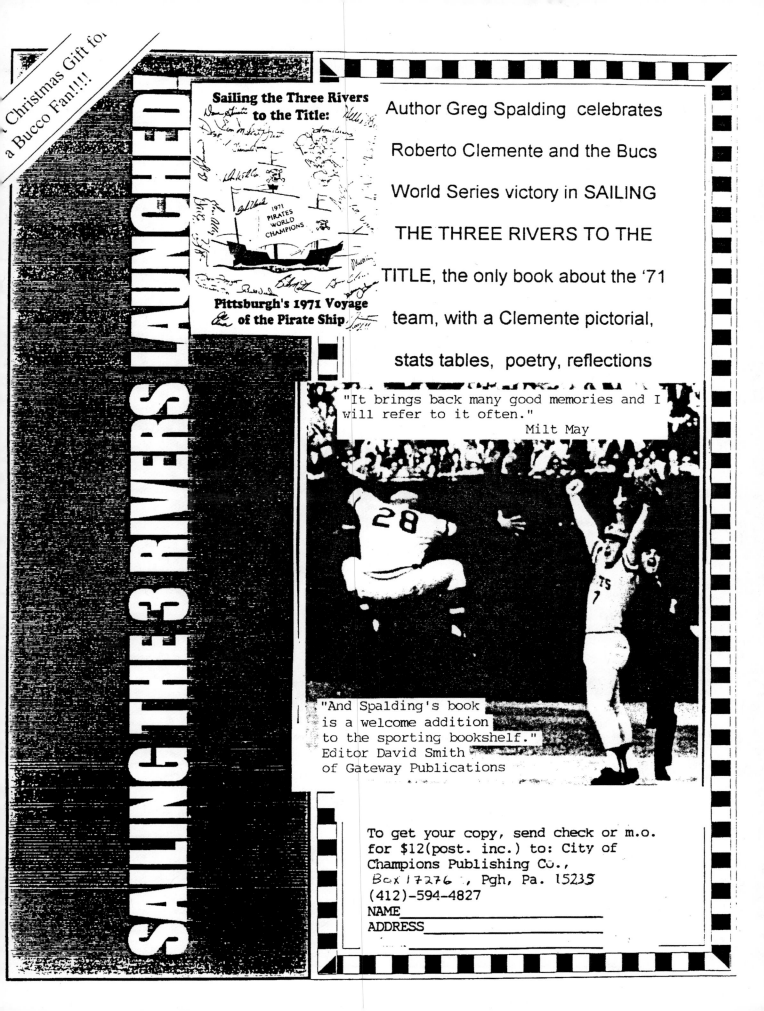

SPORTS

■ NEW AUTHOR

Tribute to 'under-rated' '71 Pirate

By David Smith

Gateway editor

The legends had long before been cast in memory.

By the summer of 1971, Bill Mazeroski had reached the twilight of a sterling defensive career, one embellished for all time by one swing taken against Ralph Terry 11 autumns before.

Roberto Clemente, the hitter and the right fielder, had reached, at least in Pittsburgh and corners of the National League, the apex of fame. Willie Stargell had stepped forward as a bonafide power threat approaching his prime.

"I really got into the team, and it is very underappreciated. I liked the personalities like Sanguillen and Al Oliver and Stargell and Clemente. I liked their character."

— Greg Spalding

Law and Groat, Skinner and Stuart, had departed. So had Forbes Field, the classic sleeveless uniforms, the distinctive black caps. In their places, a brand-new Three Rivers Stadium, double-knit pullover jerseys and an electronic scoreboard trumpeted a slick new age.

It was the age of a new group of young ballplayers — Oliver, Cash, Hebner, Robertson, Sanguillen, Stennett and others.

Far from the big league limelight, a generation of young fans who knew nothing of Vinegar Bend, of Hal Smith, of Aunt Minnie's window, were taking their turn by the crackling radio that spit Bob Prince's syrupy tones on humid summer nights.

This generation hit the sandlots whirling the bat in a Stargellesque windmill, falling off the mound like Steve Blass and mimicking the eclectic styles of Hebner and the power stroke of Robby.

Greg Spalding was one of them.

But Spalding wasn't just celebrating the 1971 Pirates in the stands and down at the local ballyard. At age 13, growing up in Penn Hills, he was remembering, and committing to print the ballteam he loved.

"I really got into the team, and it is very underappreciated," says Spalding. "I liked the personalities like Sanguillen and Al Oliver and Stargell and Clemente. I liked their character."

Spalding, 36, has released his first book, "Sailing the Three Rivers to the Title: Pittsburgh's 1971 Voyage of the

RECALLING ROBERTO Clemente, Willie Stargell, Manny Sanguillen and the Pirates of 1971, Greg Spalding has published a book celebrating a world championship team lost between Pirate glories of 1960 and 1979.

Pirate Ship." It is a book he began writing as a teen-ager watching the team.

It is a long overdue book on a team that deserves more celebration and examination.

The 1971 Pirates are, in a way, an enigma lost in history. With a wondrous mix of youth and experience, the team was one of dynastic promise left undelivered.

It was a far better team than either the one that captured the hearts of a city in 1960 or won a world championship dancing to the "We Are Family" tune in 1979. It was a team that in that championship summer 23 years ago, seemed destined to rule the baseball world for years.

But, as if by some dizzying mix of

caprice and misfortune, the team never returned to the top. Maz, Alley, Pagan, manager Danny Murtaugh and other older ingredients retired. Clemente died tragically after the 1972 season. Blass lost the stuff that made him an ace.. Robby's numbers, likewise, eventually tailed off.

While Oliver went on to smack nearly 3,000 hits in a multi-team career, only Stargell, and Bruce Kison, a '71 rookie, remained in Pittsburgh to key the '79 World Series champs under Chuck Tanner.

A baseball team has a way of impacting a youngster the most in those years when he first discovers the breadth and scope of the game. The timing was perfect for a young Spalding in '71, and he discovered a team that has stuck

with him over the years — his own "boys of summer."

He remembers Oliver and Sanguillen as personal favorites.

"Oliver just played hard every day," he says. "He hit the ball hard almost every time, and he was so much a perfectionist.

"I remember Sanguillen behind plate and how he was always smiling having a good time."

In fact, the Latin American players on that team had a deeper impact on Spalding than just runs, hits and errors. A Spanish teacher the Community College of Alleghe County, he credits his love of Sang Clemente, Vic Davalillo and other with getting him interested in the language.

He graduated from Grove City College and lives in Wilkinsburg.

Spalding's book is an easy and lively read. It is unique because it comes from purely a fan's perspective and will no doubt resurrect a sack full of memories in readers may have forgotten '71 in a time when the Bucs of '60 are remembe above all else.

"This book is the fulfillm of a baseball dream to me

— Greg Spald

He got to meet members of the team at their 20th reunion game in 1991, has talked to them at baseba card shows and other events. Gett to know the players has only deep ened his love of the '71 team that proved a lot to the baseball world

"They were really an underdog the Series against the Orioles," Spalding remembers.

He recalls with perfect clarity most dramatic moment of that Se when Robertson missed a bunt si in Game 3 and slammed a three-r homer to bring home Clemente an Stargell against the Orioles in Pitt burgh.

"This book is the fulfillment of baseball dream to me."

Clemente hit .414 in that Series solidified his stature as one of the greatest players of all time.

It was certainly a paramount summer for Pittsburgh sports.

There was no Mazeroski homer mix myth with reality. There was Forbes Field and no Yankee dyna to bowl over. But the '71 Bucs wer nonetheless, a team for the ages.

And Spalding's book is a welco addition to the sporting bookshelf

Especially since it comes right from the heart of a fan who was inspired by this team and never forgot.

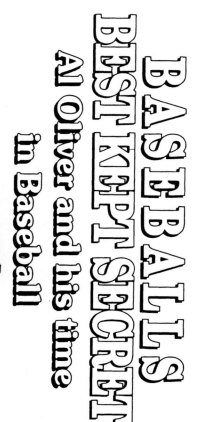

City of Champions Publishing has released *The Classiest Team Baseball Ever Knew* to commemorate the squad's 30th anniversary and the last season of both Bill Mazeroski and Roberto Clemente.

Author Greg Spalding includes:

• Day-by-day summaries of the team's regular season

• Boxscores and stories of the '72 NLCS versus the Reds

• Amazing statistics and insightful analysis

• Robertito's reflections about his father

• A tribute to "No Touch" Mazeroski

• Literary tributes to this classy team

ISBN: 1-891231-94-4

You can order *The Classiest Team Baseball Ever Knew* for only $14.95 plus $2 s/h from: City of Champions Publishing, Box 17276, Pittsburgh, PA 15235 (412-829-5042)

Name_____

Address_____

_____

Phone_____ E-mail_____

Would you like the book signed with a particular message?

_____